Department of the Treasury
Internal Revenue Service

Publication 51
Cat. No. 10320R

(Circular A), Agricultural Employer's Tax Guide

For use in **2016**

Get forms and other information faster and easier at:
- *IRS.gov* (English)   *IRS.gov/Korean* (한국어)
- *IRS.gov/Spanish* (Español) *IRS.gov/Russian* (Русский)
- *IRS.gov/Chinese* ( )   *IRS.gov/Vietnamese* (TiếngViệt)

Dec 22, 2015

Contents

Future Developments

For the latest information about developments related to Pub. 51, such as legislation enacted after it was published, go to *www.irs.gov/pub51*.

What's New

Social security and Medicare tax for 2016. The social security tax rate is 6.2% each for the employee and employer, unchanged from 2015. The social security wage base limit is $118,500, unchanged from 2015.

The Medicare tax rate is 1.45% each for the employee and employer, unchanged from 2015. There is no wage base limit for Medicare tax.

Social security and Medicare taxes apply to the wages of household workers you pay $2,000 or more in cash or an equivalent form of compensation.

2016 withholding tables. This publication includes the 2016 Percentage Method Tables and Wage Bracket Tables for Income Tax Withholding.

Withholding allowance. The 2016 amount for one withholding allowance on an annual basis is $4,050.

New filing due date for 2016 Forms W-2, W-3, and 1099-MISC. Both paper and electronically filed 2016 Forms W-2 and W-3 must be filed with the Social Security Administration (SSA) by January 31, 2017. Both paper and electronically filed 2016 Form 1099-MISC must be filed with the IRS by January 31, 2017.

Work opportunity tax credit for qualified tax-exempt organizations hiring qualified veterans extended. The work opportunity tax credit is now available for eligible unemployed veterans who begin work after December 31, 2014, and before January 1, 2020. Qualified tax-exempt organizations that hire eligible unemployed veterans can claim the work opportunity tax credit against their payroll tax liability using Form 5884-C. For more information, visit IRS.gov and enter "work opportunity tax credit" in the search box.

New Pub. 5146 explains employment tax examinations and appeal rights. Pub. 5146 provides employers with information on how the IRS selects employment tax returns to be examined, what happens during an exam, and what options an employer has in responding to the results of an exam, including how to appeal the results. Pub. 5146 also includes information on worker classification issues and tip exams.

Reminders

COBRA premium assistance credit. Effective for tax periods beginning after December 31, 2013, the credit for COBRA premium assistance payments can't be claimed on Form 943, Employer's Annual Federal Tax Return for Agricultural Employees. Instead, after filing your Form 943, file Form 943-X, Adjusted Employer's Annual Federal Tax Return for Agricultural Employees or Claim for Refund, to claim the COBRA premium assistance credit. Filing a Form 943-X before filing a Form 943 for the year may result in errors or delays in processing your Form 943-X. For more information, see the Instructions for Form 943 or visit IRS.gov and enter "COBRA" in the search box.

Same-sex marriage. For federal tax purposes, marriages of couples of the same sex are treated the same as marriages of couples of the opposite sex. The term "spouse" includes an individual married to a person of the same sex. However, individuals who have entered into a registered domestic partnership, civil union, or other similar relationship that isn't considered a marriage under state law aren't considered married for federal tax purposes. For more information, see Revenue Ruling 2013-17, 2013-38 I.R.B. 201, available at *www.irs.gov/irb/2013-38_IRB/ar07.html*.

Notice 2013-61 provides special administrative procedures for employers to make claims for refunds or adjustments of overpayments of social security and Medicare taxes with respect to certain same-sex spouse benefits before expiration of the period of limitations. Notice 2013-61, 2013-44 I.R.B. 432, is available at *www.irs.gov/irb/2013-44_IRB/ar10.html*. You may correct errors to federal income tax withholding and Additional Medicare Tax withheld for prior years if the amount reported on your employment tax return doesn't agree with the amount you actually withheld. This type of error is an administrative error. You may also correct errors to federal income tax withholding and Additional Medicare Tax withheld for prior years if section 3509 rates apply.

Additional Medicare Tax withholding. In addition to withholding Medicare tax at 1.45%, you must withhold a 0.9% Additional Medicare Tax from wages you pay to an employee in excess of $200,000 in a calendar year. You are required to begin withholding Additional Medicare Tax in the pay period in which you pay wages in excess of $200,000 to an employee and continue to withhold it each pay period until the end of the calendar year. Additional Medicare Tax is only imposed on the employee. There is no employer share of Additional Medicare Tax. All wages that are subject to Medicare tax are subject to Additional Medicare Tax withholding if paid in excess of the $200,000 withholding threshold.

For more information on what wages are subject to Medicare tax, see the chart, *Special Rules for Various Types of Services and Payments*, in section 15 of Pub. 15. For more information on Additional Medicare Tax, visit IRS.gov and enter "Additional Medicare Tax" in the search box.

Outsourcing payroll duties. You are responsible to ensure that tax returns are filed and deposits and payments are made, even if you contract with a third-party to perform these acts. You remain responsible if the third-party fails to perform any required action. If you choose to outsource any of your payroll and related tax duties (that is, withholding, reporting, and paying over social security, Medicare, FUTA, and income taxes) to a third-party payer, such as a payroll service provider or reporting agent, visit IRS.gov and enter "outsourcing payroll duties" in the search box for helpful information on this topic.

Compensation paid to H-2A foreign agricultural workers. Report compensation of $600 or more paid to foreign agricultural workers who entered the country on H-2A visas in box 1 of Form W-2, Wage and Tax Statement. Compensation paid to H-2A workers for agricultural labor performed in connection with this visa isn't subject to social security and Medicare taxes, and therefore shouldn't be reported as wages subject to social security tax (line 2), Medicare tax (line 4), or Additional Medicare Tax withholding (line 6) on Form 943, and shouldn't be reported as social security wages (box 3) or Medicare wages (box 5) on Form W-2. On Form W-2, don't check box 13 (Statutory employee), as H-2A workers aren't statutory employees.

An employer isn't required to withhold federal income tax from compensation it pays an H-2A worker for agricultural labor performed in connection with this visa but may withhold if the worker asks for withholding and the employer agrees. In that case, the worker must give the employer a completed Form W-4, Employee's Withholding Allowance Certificate. Federal income tax withheld should be reported on Form 943, line 8, and in box 2 of Form W-2.

These reporting rules apply when the H-2A worker provides his or her taxpayer identification number (TIN) to the employer. If the H-2A worker doesn't provide a TIN and the total annual wages to the H-2A worker are at least $600, the employer is required to backup withhold. See the Instructions for Form 1099-MISC and the Instructions for Form 945.

Disregarded entities and qualified subchapter S subsidiaries (QSubs). Eligible single-owner disregarded entities and QSubs are treated as separate entities for employment tax purposes. Eligible single-member entities that haven't elected to be taxed as corporations must report and pay employment taxes on wages paid to their employees using the entities' own names and EINs. See Regulations sections 1.1361-4(a)(7) and 301.7701-2(c)(2)(iv).

Differential wage payments. Qualified differential wage payments made by employers to individuals serving in the Armed Forces after 2008 are subject to income tax withholding but not social security, Medicare, or FUTA taxes. For more information, see Pub. 15.

Federal tax deposits must be made by electronic funds transfer (EFT). You must use EFT to make all federal tax deposits. Generally, an EFT is made using the Electronic Federal Tax Payment System (EFTPS). If you don't want to use EFTPS, you can arrange for your tax professional, financial institution, payroll service, or other trusted third-party to make electronic deposits on your behalf. Also, you may arrange for your financial institution to initiate a same-day wire payment on your behalf. EFTPS is a free service provided by the Department of Treasury. Services provided by your tax professional, financial institution, payroll service, or other third-party may have a fee.

For more information on making federal tax deposits, see *How To Deposit* in section 7. To get more information about EFTPS or to enroll in EFTPS, visit *www.eftps.gov* or call 1-800-555-4477 or 1-800-733-4829 (TDD). Additional information about EFTPS is also available in Pub. 966.

Electronic filing and payment. Now, more than ever before, businesses can enjoy the benefits of filing tax returns and paying their taxes electronically. Whether you rely on a tax professional or handle your own taxes, the IRS offers you convenient programs to make it easier.

Spend less time and worry on taxes and more time running your business. Use *e-file* and EFTPS to your benefit.

- For *e-file*, visit the IRS website at *www.irs.gov/efile* for additional information.

- For EFTPS, visit *www.eftps.gov* or call EFTPS Customer Service at 1-800-555-4477 or 1-800-733-4829 (TDD) for additional information.

- For electronic filing of Form W-2, visit *www.socialsecurity.gov/employer*.

![CAUTION] *If you are filing your tax return or paying your federal taxes electronically, a valid EIN is required. If a valid EIN isn't provided, the return or payment won't be processed. This may result in penalties and delays in processing your return or payment.*

Electronic funds withdrawal (EFW). If you file Form 943 electronically, you can *e-file* and e-pay (electronic funds withdrawal) the balance due in a single step using tax preparation software or through a tax professional. However, don't use EFW to make federal tax deposits. For more information on paying your taxes using EFW, visit the IRS website at *www.irs.gov/payments*. A fee may be charged to file electronically.

Credit or debit card payments. Employers can pay the balance due shown on Form 943 by credit or debit card. Don't use a credit or debit card to make federal tax deposits. For more information on paying your taxes with a credit or debit card, visit the IRS website at *www.irs.gov/payments*.

Online payment agreement. You may be eligible to apply for an installment agreement online if you have a balance due when you file your employment tax return. For more information, see the instructions for your employment tax return or visit the IRS website at *www.irs.gov/payments*.

When you hire a new employee. Ask each new employee to complete the 2016 Form W-4, or its Spanish version, Formulario W-4(SP). Also, ask the employee to show you his or her social security card so that you can record the employee's name and social security number (SSN) accurately. If the employee has lost the card or recently changed names, have the employee apply for a duplicate or corrected card. If the employee doesn't have a card, have the employee apply for one on Form SS-5, Application for a Social Security Card. See section 1 for more information.

Eligibility for employment. You must verify that each new employee is legally eligible to work in the United States. This includes completing the U.S. Citizenship and Immigration Services (USCIS) Form I-9, Employment Eligibility Verification. You can get Form I-9 at *www.uscis.gov/forms*, USCIS offices, or by calling 1-800-870-3676. For more information, visit the USCIS website at *www.uscis.gov* or call 1-800-375-5283 or 1-800-767-1833 (TDD).

New hire reporting. You are required to report any new employee to a designated state new-hire registry. A new employee is an employee who hasn't previously been employed by you or was previously employed by you but has been separated from such prior employment for at least 60 consecutive days. Many states accept a copy of Form W-4 with employer information added. Visit the Office of Child Support Enforcement's website at *www.acf.hhs.gov/programs/cse/newhire* for more information.

Dishonored payments. Any form of payment that is dishonored and returned from a financial institution is subject to a penalty. The penalty is $25 or 2% of the payment, whichever is more. However, the penalty on dishonored payments of $24.99 or less is an amount equal to the payment. For example, a dishonored payment of $18 is charged a penalty of $18.

Forms in Spanish. You can provide Formulario W-4(SP) in place of Form W-4 to your Spanish-speaking employees. For more information, see Pub. 17(SP), El Impuesto Federal sobre los Ingresos (Para Personas Físicas).

For nonemployees, Formulario W-9(SP), Solicitud y Certificación del Número de Identificación del Contribuyente, may be used in place of Form W-9, Request for Taxpayer Identification Number and Certification.

References in this publication to Form W-4 or Form W-9 also apply to their equivalent Spanish translations—Formulario W-4(SP) or Formulario W-9(SP).

Information returns. You may be required to file information returns to report certain types of payments made during the year. For example, you must file Form 1099-MISC, Miscellaneous Income, to report payments of $600 or more to persons not treated as employees (for example, independent contractors) for services performed for your trade or business. For details about filing Forms 1099 and for information about required electronic filing, see the General Instructions for Certain Information Returns for general information and the separate, specific instructions for each information return that you file (for example, Instructions for Form 1099-MISC). Generally, don't use Forms 1099 to report wages or other compensation that you paid to employees; report these amounts on Form W-2.

See the General Instructions for Forms W-2 and W-3 for details about filing Forms W-2 and for information about required electronic filing. If you file 250 or more Forms W-2, you must file them electronically. The IRS and Social Security Administration (SSA) won't accept information returns on magnetic media.

Information reporting customer service site. The IRS operates an information return customer service site to answer questions about reporting on Forms W-2, W-3, 1099, and other information returns. If you have questions related to reporting on information returns, you may call 1-866-455-7438 (toll free), 304-263-8700 (toll call), or 304-579-4827 (TDD/TTY for persons who are deaf, hard of hearing, or have a speech disability). The call site can also be reached by email at *mccirp@irs.gov*. Don't include tax identification numbers (TINs) or attachments in email correspondence because electronic mail isn't secure.

Web-based application for an employer identification number (EIN). You can apply for an EIN online. Go to IRS.gov and enter "EIN" in the search box.

When a crew leader furnishes workers to you. Record the crew leader's name, address, and EIN. See sections 2 and 10.

Change of address. Use Form 8822-B to notify the IRS of an address change. Don't mail form 8822-B with your employment tax return.

Change of responsible party. Any entity with an EIN must file Form 8822-B to report the latest change to its responsible party. Form 8822-B must be filed within 60 days of the change. For a definition of "responsible party," see the Form 8822-B instructions.

Ordering forms and publications. You can order employment tax and information return forms, instructions, and publications online at *www.irs.gov/orderforms*. You can also visit *www.irs.gov/formspubs* to download forms, instructions, and publications.

Instead of ordering paper Forms W-2 and W-3, consider filing them electronically using the SSA's free *e-file* service. Visit the SSA's Employer W-2 Filing Instructions & Information website at *www.socialsecurity.gov/employer*, to register for Business Services Online. You will be able to create and file "fill-in" versions of Forms W-2 with SSA and can print out completed copies of Forms W-2 for filing with state and local governments, distribution to your employees, and for your records. Form W-3 will be created for you based on your Forms W-2.

Tax questions. If you have an employment tax question, check the information available on IRS.gov or call 1-800-829-4933 or 1-800-829-4059 (TDD/TTY for persons who are deaf, hard of hearing, or have a speech disability) Monday–Friday from 7:00 a.m.–7:00 p.m. local time (Alaska and Hawaii follow Pacific time). We can't answer tax questions sent to the address provided later for comments and suggestions.

Recordkeeping. Keep all records of employment taxes for at least 4 years. These should be available for IRS review. Your records should include the following information.

- Your EIN.

- Amounts and dates of all wage, annuity, and pension payments.

- Names, addresses, SSNs, and occupations of employees and recipients.

- Any employee copies of Forms W-2 and W-2c returned to you as undeliverable.

- Dates of employment for each employee.

- Periods for which employees and recipients were paid while absent due to sickness or injury and the amount and weekly rate of payments you or third-party payers made to them.

- Copies of employees' and recipients' income tax withholding allowance certificates (Forms W-4, W-4(SP), W-4P, and W-4S).

- Dates and amounts of tax deposits you made and acknowledgment numbers for deposits made by EFTPS.

- Copies of returns filed and confirmation numbers.

- Records of fringe benefits and expense reimbursements provided to your employees, including substantiation.

If a crew leader furnished you with farmworkers, you must keep a record of the name, permanent mailing address, and EIN of the crew leader. If the crew leader has no permanent mailing address, record his or her present address.

Private delivery services. You can use certain private delivery services designated by the IRS to send tax returns and payments. The list includes only the following.

- Federal Express (FedEx): FedEx First Overnight, FedEx Priority Overnight, FedEx Standard Overnight, FedEx 2 Day, FedEx International Next Flight Out, FedEx International Priority, FedEx International First, and FedEx International Economy.

- United Parcel Service (UPS): UPS Next Day Air Early AM, UPS Next Day Air, UPS Next Day Air Saver, UPS 2nd Day Air, UPS 2nd Day Air A.M., UPS Worldwide Express Plus, and UPS Worldwide Express.

For the IRS mailing address to use if you are using a private delivery service, go to IRS.gov and enter "private delivery service" in the search box.

Your private delivery service can tell you how to get written proof of the mailing date.

 Private delivery services can't deliver items to P.O. boxes. You must use the U.S. Postal Service to mail any item to an IRS P.O. box address.

Photographs of missing children. The IRS is a proud partner with the National Center for Missing and Exploited Children. Photographs of missing children selected by the Center may appear in this publication on pages that would otherwise be blank. You can help bring these children home by looking at the photographs and calling 1-800-THE-LOST (1-800-843-5678) if you recognize a child.

Calendar

The following are important dates and responsibilities. See section 7 for information about depositing taxes reported on Forms 941, 943, 944, and 945. Also see Pub. 509, Tax Calendars.

 If any date shown below for filing a return, furnishing a form, or depositing taxes falls on a Saturday, Sunday, or legal holiday, the due date is the next business day. A statewide legal holiday delays a filing due date only if the IRS office where you are required to file is located in that state. However, a statewide legal holiday doesn't delay the due date of federal tax deposits. See Deposits on Business Days Only in section 7. For any filing due date, you will meet the "file" or "furnish" requirement if the envelope containing the return or form is properly addressed, contains sufficient postage, and is postmarked by the U.S. Postal Service on or before the due date, or sent by an IRS-designated delivery service on or before the due date. See Private delivery services under Reminders.

By January 31

- File Form 943. See section 8 for more information on Form 943. If you deposited all Form 943 taxes when due, you may file Form 943 by February 10.

- Furnish each employee with a completed Form W-2.

- Furnish each recipient to whom you paid $600 or more in nonemployee compensation with a completed Form 1099 (for example, Form 1099-MISC).

- File Form 940, Employer's Annual Federal Unemployment (FUTA) Tax Return. See section 10 for more information on FUTA. If you deposited all the FUTA tax when due, you may file Form 940 by February 10.

- File Form 945, Annual Return of Withheld Federal Income Tax, to report any nonpayroll federal income tax withheld in 2015. If you deposited all Form 945 taxes when due, you may file Form 945 by February 10.

By February 15

Ask for a new Form W-4 or Formulario W-4(SP) from each employee who claimed exemption from federal income tax withholding last year.

On February 16

Any Form W-4 claiming exemption from withholding for the previous year has now expired. Begin withholding for any employee who previously claimed exemption from withholding but hasn't given you a new Form W-4 for the current year. If the employee doesn't give you a new Form W-4, withhold tax based on the last valid Form W-4 you have for the employee that doesn't claim exemption from withholding or, if one doesn't exist, as if he or she is single with zero withholding allowances. See section 5 for more information. If the employee furnishes a new Form W-4 claiming exemption from withholding after February 15, you may apply the exemption to future wages, but don't refund taxes withheld while the exempt status wasn't in place.

 Both paper and electronically filed 2016 Forms W-2 and W-3 must be filed with the SSA by January 31, 2017. Both paper and electronically filed 2016 Form 1099-MISC must be filed with the IRS by January 31, 2017.

By February 28

File paper 2015 Forms 1099 and 1096. File Copy A of all paper 2015 Forms 1099 with Form 1096, Annual Summary and Transmittal of U.S. Information Returns, with the IRS. For electronically filed returns, see By March 31 below.

By February 29

File paper 2015 Forms W-2 and W-3. File Copy A of all paper 2015 Forms W-2 with Form W-3, Transmittal of Wage and Tax Statements, with the SSA. For electronically filed returns, see By March 31 next.

By March 31

File electronic 2015 Forms W-2 and 1099. File electronic 2015 Forms W-2 with the SSA and 2015 Forms 1099 with the IRS. For more information on reporting Form W-2 information to the SSA electronically, visit the SSA's Employer W-2 Filing Instructions & Information webpage at www.socialsecurity.gov/employer. For information on filing information returns electronically with the IRS, see Pub. 1220.

By April 30, July 31, October 31, and January 31

Deposit FUTA taxes. Deposit FUTA tax if the undeposited amount is over $500.

Before December 1

Remind employees to submit a new Form W-4 if their marital status or withholding allowances have changed or will change for the next year.

Introduction

This publication is for employers of agricultural workers (farmworkers). It contains information that you may need to comply with the laws for agricultural labor (farmwork) relating to social security and Medicare taxes, FUTA tax, and withheld federal income tax (employment taxes). Agricultural employers report social security and Medicare taxes and withheld federal income tax on Form 943 and report FUTA tax on Form 940.

When you pay your employees, you don't pay them all the money they earned. As their employer, you have the added responsibility of withholding taxes from their paychecks. The federal income tax and employees' share of social security and Medicare taxes that you withhold from your employees' paychecks are part of their wages that you pay to the United States Treasury instead of to your employees. Your employees trust that you pay the withheld taxes to the United States Treasury by making federal tax deposits. This is the reason that these withheld taxes are called trust fund taxes. If federal income, social security, or Medicare taxes that must be withheld aren't withheld or aren't deposited or paid to the United States Treasury, the trust fund recovery penalty may apply. See section 7 for more information.

If you have nonfarm employees, see Pub. 15. If you have employees in the U.S. Virgin Islands, Guam, American Samoa, or the Commonwealth of the Northern Mariana Islands, see Pub. 80. Pub. 15-A contains more employment-related information, including information about sick pay and pension income. Pub. 15-B contains information about the employment tax treatment and valuation of various types of noncash compensation.

Comments and suggestions. We welcome your comments about this publication and your suggestions for future editions.

You can send us comments from *www.irs.gov/formspubs*. Click on *More Information* and then click on *Give us feedback*.

Or you can write to:

Internal Revenue Service
Tax Forms and Publications
1111 Constitution Ave. NW, IR-6526
Washington, DC 20224

We respond to many letters by telephone. Therefore, it would be helpful if you would include your daytime phone number, including the area code, in your correspondence.

Although we can't respond individually to each email, we do appreciate your feedback and will consider your comments as we revise our forms, instructions, and publications.

COBRA premium assistance credit. The Consolidated Omnibus Budget Reconciliation Act of 1985 (COBRA) provides certain former employees, retirees, spouses, former spouses, and dependent children the right to temporary continuation of health coverage at group rates. COBRA generally covers multiemployer health plans and health plans maintained by private-sector employers (other than churches) with 20 or more full and part-time employees. Parallel requirements apply to these plans under the Employee Retirement Income Security Act of 1974 (ERISA). Under the Public Health Service Act, COBRA requirements apply also to health plans covering state or local government employees. Similar requirements apply under the Federal Employees Health Benefits Program and under some state laws. For the premium assistance (or subsidy) discussed below, these requirements are all referred to as COBRA requirements.

Under the American Recovery and Reinvestment Act of 2009 (ARRA), employers are allowed a credit against "payroll taxes" (referred to in this publication as "employment taxes") for providing COBRA premium assistance to assistance eligible individuals. For periods of COBRA continuation coverage beginning after February 16, 2009, a group health plan must treat an assistance eligible individual as having paid the required COBRA continuation coverage premium if the individual elects COBRA coverage and pays 35% of the amount of the premium.

An assistance eligible individual is a qualified beneficiary of an employer's group health plan who is eligible for COBRA continuation coverage during the period beginning September 1, 2008, and ending May 31, 2010, due to the involuntary termination from employment of a covered employee during the period and elects continuation COBRA coverage. The assistance for the coverage can last up to 15 months.

Employees terminated during the period beginning September 1, 2008, and ending May 31, 2010, who received a severance package that delayed the start of the COBRA continuation coverage, may still be eligible for premium assistance for COBRA continuation coverage. For more information, see Notice 2009-27, 2009-16 I.R.B. 838, available at *www.irs.gov/irb/2009-16_irb/ar09.html*.

Administrators of the group health plans (or other entities) that provide or administer COBRA continuation coverage must provide notice to assistance eligible individuals of the COBRA premium assistance.

The 65% of the premium not paid by the assistance eligible individual is reimbursed to the employer maintaining the group health plan. The reimbursement is made through a credit against the employer's employment tax liabilities. For information on how to claim the credit, see the Instructions for Form 943-X. The credit is treated as a deposit made on the first day of the return period. In the case of a multiemployer plan, the credit is claimed by the plan, rather than the employer. In the case of an insured plan subject to state law continuation coverage requirements, the credit is claimed by the insurance company, rather than the employer.

Anyone claiming the credit for COBRA premium assistance payments must maintain the following information to support their claim.

- Information on the receipt of the assistance eligible individuals' 35% share of the premium, including dates and amounts.

- In the case of an insurance plan, a copy of invoice or other supporting statement from the insurance carrier and proof of timely payment of the full premium to the insurance carrier required under COBRA.

- In the case of a self-insured plan, proof of the premium amount and proof of the coverage provided to the assistance eligible individuals.

- Attestation of involuntary termination, including the date of the involuntary termination for each covered employee whose involuntary termination is the basis for eligibility for the subsidy.

- Proof of each assistance eligible individual's eligibility for COBRA coverage and the election of COBRA coverage.

- A record of the SSNs of all covered employees, the amount of the subsidy reimbursed with respect to each covered employee, and whether the subsidy was for one individual or two or more individuals.

For more information, visit IRS.gov and enter "COBRA" in the search box.

Useful Items

You may want to see:

Publication

- ❏ **15** Employer's Tax Guide
- ❏ **15-A** Employer's Supplemental Tax Guide
- ❏ **15-B** Employer's Tax Guide to Fringe Benefits
- ❏ **225** Farmer's Tax Guide
- ❏ **535** Business Expenses
- ❏ **583** Starting a Business and Keeping Records
- ❏ **1635** Employer Identification Number: Understanding Your EIN

1. Taxpayer Identification Numbers

If you are required to withhold any federal income, social security, or Medicare taxes, you will need an EIN for yourself. Also, you will need the SSN of each employee and the name of each employee as shown on the employee's social security card.

Employer identification number (EIN). An EIN is a nine-digit number that the IRS issues. The digits are arranged as follows: 00-0000000. It is used to identify the tax accounts of employers and certain others who have no employees. Use your EIN on all of the items that you send to the IRS and SSA.

If you don't have an EIN, you may apply for one online. Go to IRS.gov and enter "EIN" in the search box. You may also apply for an EIN by faxing or mailing Form SS-4 to the IRS. Don't use an SSN in place of an EIN.

If you don't have an EIN by the time a return is due, write "Applied For" and the date you applied for it in the space shown for the number. If you took over another employer's business, don't use that employer's EIN.

You should have only one EIN. If you have more than one, and aren't sure which one to use, call the toll-free Business and Specialty Tax Line at 1-800-829-4933 or 1-800-829-4059 (TDD/TTY for persons who are deaf, hard of hearing, or have a speech disability). Provide the EINs that you have, the name and address to which each number was assigned, and the address of your principal place of business. The IRS will tell you which EIN to use.

For more information, see Pub. 1635 or Pub. 583.

When you receive your EIN. If you are a new employer that indicated a federal tax obligation when requesting an EIN, you will be pre-enrolled in EFTPS. You will receive information in your EIN Package about Express Enrollment and an additional mailing containing your EFTPS personal identification number (PIN) and instructions for activating your PIN. Call the toll-free number located in your "How to Activate Your Enrollment" brochure to activate your enrollment and begin making your employment tax deposits. If you outsource any of your payroll and related tax duties to a third-party payer, such as a payroll service provider or reporting agent, be sure to tell them about your EFTPS enrollment.

Social security number (SSN). An employee's SSN consists of nine digits arranged as follows: 000-00-0000. You must obtain each employee's name and SSN as shown on the employee's social security card because you must enter them on Form W-2. Don't accept a social security card that says "Not valid for employment." A social security number issued with this legend doesn't permit employment. You may, but aren't required to, photocopy the social security card if the employee provides it. If you don't show the employee's correct name and SSN on Form W-2, you may owe a penalty unless you have reasonable cause. See Pub. 1586, Reasonable Cause Regulations & Requirements for Missing and Incorrect Name/TINs.

Applying for a social security card. Any employee who is legally eligible to work in the United States and doesn't have a social security card can get one by completing Form SS-5 and submitting the necessary documentation to the SSA. You can get Form SS-5 at *www.socialsecurity.gov/online/ss-5.html*, SSA offices, or by calling 1-800-772-1213 or 1-800-325-0778 (TTY). The employee must complete and sign Form SS-5; it can't be filed by the employer. You may be asked to supply a letter to accompany Form SS-5 if the employee has exceeded his or her yearly or lifetime limit for the number of replacement cards allowed.

Applying for an SSN. If you file Form W-2 on paper and your employee has applied for an SSN but doesn't have one when you must file Form W-2, enter "Applied For" on the form. If you are filing electronically, enter all zeros (000-00-0000) in the SSN field. When the employee receives the SSN, file Copy A of Form W-2c, Corrected Wage and Tax Statement, with the SSA to show the employee's SSN. Furnish Copies B, C, and 2 of Form W-2c to the employee. Up to 25 Forms W-2c per Form W-3c, Transmittal of Corrected Wage and Tax Statements, may be filed per session over the Internet, with no limit on the number of sessions. For more information, visit SSA's Employer W-2 Filing Instructions & Information webpage at *www.socialsecurity.gov/employer*. Advise your employee to correct the SSN on his or her original Form W-2.

Correctly record the employee's name and SSN. Record the name and SSN of each employee as they are shown on the employee's social security card. If the employee's name isn't correct as shown on the card (for example, because of marriage or divorce), the employee should request an updated card from the SSA. Continue to report the employee's wages under the old name until the employee shows you an updated social security card with the new name.

If the SSA issues the employee an updated card after a name change, or a new card with a different SSN, file a Form W-2c to correct the name/SSN reported on the most recently filed Form W-2. It isn't necessary to correct other years if the previous name and SSN were used for years before the most recent Form W-2.

IRS individual taxpayer identification numbers (ITINs) for aliens. Don't accept an ITIN in place of an SSN for employee identification or for work. An ITIN is issued for use by resident and nonresident aliens who need identification for tax purposes, but who aren't eligible for U.S. employment. You can identify an ITIN because it is a nine-digit number, formatted like an SSN, that starts with the number "9" and has a range of numbers from "70-88," "90-92," and "94-99" for the fourth and fifth digits (for example, 9NN-7N-NNNN).

 An individual with an ITIN who later becomes eligible to work in the United States must obtain an SSN. If the individual is currently eligible to work in the United States, instruct the individual to apply for an SSN and follow the instructions under Applying for an SSN, *earlier in this section. Don't use an ITIN in place of an SSN on Form W-2.*

Verification of SSNs. Employers and authorized reporting agents can use the Social Security Number Verification Service (SSNVS) to instantly verify up to 10 employee names and SSNs (per screen) at a time, or submit an electronic file of up to 250,000 names and SSNs and usually receive results the next business day. Visit *www.socialsecurity.gov/employer/ssnv.htm* for more information.

Registering for SSNVS. You must register online and receive authorization from your employer to use SSNVS. To register, visit SSA's website at *www.socialsecurity.gov/bso* and click on the *Register* link under *Business Services Online*. Follow the registration instructions to obtain a user identification (ID) and password. You will need to provide the following information about yourself and your company.

- Name.

- SSN.

- Date of birth.

- Type of employer.

- EIN.

- Company name, address, and telephone number.

- Email address.

When you have completed the online registration process, SSA will mail a one-time activation code to your employer. You must enter the activation code online to use SSNVS.

2. Who Are Employees?

Generally, employees are defined either under common law or under statutes for certain situations. See Pub. 15-A for details on statutory employees and nonemployees.

Employee status under common law. Generally, a worker who performs services for you is your employee if you have the right to control what will be done and how it will be done. This is so even when you give the employee freedom of action. What matters is that you have the right to control the details of how the services are performed. See Pub. 15-A for more information on how to determine whether an individual providing services is an independent contractor or an employee.

If an employer-employee relationship exists, it doesn't matter what it is called. The employee may be called an agent or independent contractor. It also doesn't matter how payments are measured or paid, what they are called, or if the employee works full or part time.

You are responsible for withholding and paying employment taxes for your employees. You are also required to file employment tax returns. These requirements don't apply to amounts that you pay to independent contractors. The rules discussed in this publication apply only to workers who are your employees.

In general, you are an employer of farmworkers if your employees:

- Raise or harvest agricultural or horticultural products on your farm (including the raising and feeding of livestock);

- Work in connection with the operation, management, conservation, improvement, or maintenance of your farm and its tools and equipment;

- Provide services relating to salvaging timber, or clearing land of brush and other debris, left by a hurricane (also known as hurricane labor), if the major part of such service is performed on a farm;

- Handle, process, or package any agricultural or horticultural commodity if you produced over half of the commodity (for a group of up to 20 unincorporated operators, all of the commodity); or

- Do work for you related to cotton ginning, turpentine, gum resin products, or the operation and maintenance of irrigation facilities.

For this purpose, the term "farm" includes stock, dairy, poultry, fruit, fur-bearing animals, and truck farms, as well as plantations, ranches, nurseries, ranges, greenhouses or other similar structures used primarily for the raising of agricultural or horticultural commodities, and orchards.

Farmwork doesn't include reselling activities that don't involve any substantial activity of raising agricultural or horticultural commodities, such as a retail store or a greenhouse used primarily for display or storage.

The table in section 12, *How Do Employment Taxes Apply to Farmwork*, distinguishes between farm and nonfarm activities, and also addresses rules that apply in special situations.

Crew Leaders

If you are a crew leader, you are an employer of farmworkers. A crew leader is a person who furnishes and pays (either on his or her own behalf or on behalf of the farm operator) workers to do farmwork for the farm operator. If there is no written agreement between you and the farm operator stating that you are his or her employee and if you pay the workers (either for yourself or for the farm operator), then you are a crew leader. For FUTA tax rules, see section 10.

Business Owned and Operated by Spouses

If you and your spouse jointly own and operate a farm or nonfarm business and share in the profits and losses, you are partners in a partnership, whether or not you have a formal partnership agreement. See Pub. 541 for more details. The partnership is considered the employer of any employees, and is liable for any employment taxes due on wages paid to its employees.

Exception—Qualified joint venture. For tax years beginning after December 31, 2006, the Small Business and Work Opportunity Tax Act of 2007 (Public Law 110-28) provides that a "qualified joint venture," whose only members are spouses filing a joint income tax return, can elect not to be treated as a partnership for federal tax purposes. A qualified joint venture conducts a trade or business where:

- The only members of the joint venture are spouses who file a joint income tax return,

- Both spouses materially participate (see *Material participation* in the Instructions for Schedule C (Form 1040), line G) in the trade or business (mere joint ownership of property isn't enough),

- Both spouses elect to not be treated as a partnership, and

- The business is co-owned by both spouses and isn't held in the name of a state law entity such as a partnership or limited liability company (LLC).

To make the election, all items of income, gain, loss, deduction, and credit must be divided between the spouses, in accordance with each spouse's interest in the venture, and reported on separate Schedules C or F as sole proprietors. Each spouse must also file a separate Schedule SE to pay self-employment taxes, as applicable.

Spouses using the qualified joint venture rules are treated as sole proprietors for federal tax purposes and generally don't need an EIN. If employment taxes are owed by the qualified joint venture, either spouse may report and pay the employment taxes due on the wages paid to the employees using the EIN of that spouse's sole proprietorship. Generally, filing as a qualified joint venture won't increase the spouses' total tax owed on the joint income tax return. However, it gives each spouse credit for social security earnings on which retirement benefits are based and for Medicare coverage without filing a partnership return.

Note. If your spouse is your employee, not your partner, you must pay social security and Medicare taxes for him or her.

For more information on qualified joint ventures, visit IRS.gov and enter "qualified joint venture" in the search box.

Exception—Community income. If you and your spouse wholly own an unincorporated business as community property under the community property laws of a state, foreign country, or U.S. possession, you can treat the business either as a sole proprietorship (of the spouse who carried on the business) or a partnership. You may still make an election to be taxed as a qualified joint venture instead of a partnership. See *Exception—Qualified joint venture*, earlier in this section.

---

3. Wages and Other Compensation

Cash wages that you pay to employees for farmwork are generally subject to social security tax and Medicare tax. You may also be required to withhold, deposit, and report Additional Medicare Tax. See section 4 for more information. If the wages are subject to social security and Medicare taxes, they are also subject to federal income tax withholding. You may also be liable for FUTA tax, which isn't withheld by you or paid by the employee. FUTA tax is discussed in section 10. Cash wages include checks, money orders, etc. Don't count as cash wages the value of food, lodging, and other noncash items.

For more information on what payments are considered taxable wages, see Pub. 15.

Commodity wages. Commodity wages aren't cash and aren't subject to social security and Medicare taxes or federal income tax withholding. However, noncash payments, including commodity wages, are treated as cash wages if the substance of the transaction is a cash payment. These noncash payments are subject to social security and Medicare taxes and federal income tax withholding.

Other compensation. Pubs. 15-A and 15-B discuss other forms of compensation that may be taxable.

Family members. Generally, the wages that you pay to family members who are your employees are subject to social security and Medicare taxes, federal income tax withholding, and FUTA tax. However, certain exemptions may apply for your child, spouse, or parent. See the table, *How Do Employment Taxes Apply to Farmwork*, in section 12.

Household employees. The wages of an employee who performs household services, such as a maid, babysitter, gardener, or cook, in your home aren't subject to social security and Medicare taxes if you pay that employee cash wages of less than $2,000 in 2016.

Social security and Medicare taxes don't apply to cash wages for housework in your private home if it was done by your spouse or your child under age 21. Nor do the taxes apply to housework done by your parent unless:

- You have a child living in your home who is under age 18 or has a physical or mental condition that requires care by an adult for at least 4 continuous weeks in a calendar quarter, and

- You are a widow or widower, or divorced and not remarried, or have a spouse in the home who, because of a physical or mental condition, can't care for your child for at least 4 continuous weeks in the quarter.

For more information, see Pub. 926.

 Wages for household work may not be a deductible farm expense. See Pub. 225.

Share farmers. You don't have to withhold or pay social security and Medicare taxes on amounts paid to share farmers under share-farming arrangements.

Compensation paid to H-2A visa holders. Report compensation of $600 or more paid to foreign agricultural workers who entered the country on H-2A visas in box 1 of Form W-2 but don't report it as social security wages (box 3) or Medicare wages (box 5) on Form W-2 because compensation paid to H-2A workers for agricultural labor performed in connection with this visa isn't subject to social security and Medicare taxes. On Form W-2, don't check box 13 (Statutory employee), as H-2A workers aren't statutory employees.

An employer isn't required to withhold federal income tax from compensation it pays an H-2A worker for agricultural labor performed in connection with this visa but may withhold if the worker asks for withholding and the employer agrees. In that case, the worker must give the employer a completed Form W-4. Federal income tax withheld should be reported in box 2 of Form W-2.

These reporting rules apply when the H-2A worker provides his or her TIN to the employer. If the H-2A worker doesn't provide a TIN and the total annual wages to the H-2A worker are at least $600, the employer is required to backup withhold. See the Instructions for Form 1099-MISC and the Instructions for Form 945.

4. Social Security and Medicare Taxes

Generally, you must withhold social security and Medicare taxes on all cash wage payments that you make to your employees. You may also be required to withhold Additional Medicare Tax. For more information, see *Additional Medicare Tax withholding*, later.

The $150 Test or the $2,500 Test

All cash wages that you pay to an employee during the year for farmwork are subject to social security and Medicare taxes and federal income tax withholding if either of the two tests below is met.

- You pay cash wages to an employee of $150 or more in a year for farmwork (count all cash wages paid on a time, piecework, or other basis). The $150 test applies separately to each farmworker that you employ. If you employ a family of workers, each member is treated separately. Don't count wages paid by other employers.

- The total that you pay for farmwork (cash and noncash) to all your employees is $2,500 or more during the year.

Exceptions. The $150 and $2,500 tests don't apply to wages that you pay to a farmworker who receives less than $150 in annual cash wages and the wages aren't subject to social security and Medicare taxes, or federal income tax withholding, even if you pay $2,500 or more in that year to all of your farmworkers if the farmworker:

- Is employed in agriculture as a hand-harvest laborer,

- Is paid piece rates in an operation that is usually paid on a piece-rate basis in the region of employment,

- Commutes daily from his or her permanent home to the farm, and

- Had been employed in agriculture less than 13 weeks in the preceding calendar year.

Amounts that you pay to these seasonal farmworkers, however, count toward the $2,500-or-more test to determine whether wages that you pay to other farmworkers are subject to social security and Medicare taxes.

Social Security and Medicare Tax Withholding

The social security tax rate is 6.2%, for both the employee and employer, on the first $118,500 paid to each employee. You must withhold at this rate from each employee and pay a matching amount. The Medicare tax rate is 1.45% each for the employee and employer on all wages. You must withhold at this rate from each employee and pay a matching amount. There is no wage base limit for Medicare tax; all covered wages are subject to Medicare tax.

Social security and Medicare taxes apply to most payments of sick pay, including payments made by third parties such as insurance companies. For details, see Pub. 15-A.

Additional Medicare Tax withholding. In addition to withholding Medicare tax at 1.45%, you must withhold a 0.9% Additional Medicare Tax from wages you pay to an employee in excess of $200,000 in a calendar year. You are required to begin withholding Additional Medicare Tax in the pay period in which you pay wages in excess of $200,000 to an employee and continue to withhold it each pay period until the end of the calendar year. Additional Medicare Tax is only imposed on the employee. There is no employer share of Additional Medicare Tax. All wages that are subject to Medicare tax are subject to Additional Medicare Tax withholding if paid in excess of the $200,000 withholding threshold.

For more information on what wages are subject to Medicare tax, see the chart, *Special Rules for Various Types of Services and Payments*, in section 15 of Pub. 15. For more information on Additional Medicare Tax, visit IRS.gov and enter "Additional Medicare Tax" in the search box.

Employee share paid by employer. If you would rather pay a household or agricultural employee's share of the social security and Medicare taxes without withholding them from his or her wages, you may do so. If you don't withhold the taxes, however, you must still pay them. Any **employee** social security and Medicare taxes that you pay is additional income to the employee. Include it in box 1 of the employee's Form W-2, but don't count it as social security and Medicare wages and don't include it in boxes 3 and 5. Also, don't count the additional income as wages for FUTA tax purposes. Different rules apply to employer payments of social security and Medicare taxes for non-household and non-agricultural employees. See section 7 of Pub. 15-A.

Withholding social security and Medicare taxes on nonresident alien employees. In general, if you pay wages to nonresident alien employees, you must withhold social security and Medicare taxes as you would for a U.S. citizen or resident alien. However, see Pub. 515 for exceptions to this general rule. Also see *Compensation paid to H-2A visa holders* in section 3.

Religious exemption. An exemption from social security and Medicare taxes is available to members of a recognized religious sect opposed to public insurance. This exemption is available only if both the employee and the employer are members of the sect. For more information, see Pub. 517.

5. Federal Income Tax Withholding

Farmers and crew leaders must withhold federal income tax from the wages of farmworkers if the wages are subject to social security and Medicare taxes. The amount to withhold is figured on gross wages before taking out social security and Medicare taxes, union dues, insurance, etc. You may use one of several methods to determine the amount of federal income tax withholding. They are discussed in section 13.

Form W-4. To know how much federal income tax to withhold from employees' wages, you should have a Form W-4 on file for each employee. Encourage your employees to file an updated Form W-4 for 2016, especially if they owed taxes or received a large refund when filing their 2015 tax return. Advise your employees to use the IRS Withholding Calculator on the IRS website at *www.irs.gov/individuals* for help in determining how many withholding allowances to claim on their Form W-4.

Ask each new employee to give you a signed Form W-4 when starting work. Make the form effective with the first wage payment. If a new employee doesn't give you a completed Form W-4, withhold tax as if he or she is single, with no withholding allowances.

Forms in Spanish. You can provide Formulario W-4(SP) in place of Form W-4 to your Spanish-speaking employees. For more information, see Pub. 17(SP).

Effective date of Form W-4. A Form W-4 remains in effect until the employee gives you a new one. When you receive a new Form W-4, don't adjust withholding for pay periods before the effective date of the new form. Don't adjust withholding retroactively. If an employee gives you a replacement Form W-4, begin withholding no later than the start of the first payroll period ending on or after the 30th day from the date when you received the replacement Form W-4. For exceptions, see *Exemption from federal income tax withholding*, *IRS review of requested Forms W-4*, and *Invalid Forms W-4*, later in this section.

 A Form W-4 that makes a change for the next calendar year won't take effect in the current calendar year.

Completing Form W-4. The amount of federal income tax withholding is based on marital status and withholding allowances. Your employees may not base their withholding amounts on a fixed dollar amount or percentage. However, the employee may specify a dollar amount to be withheld in addition to the amount of withholding based on filing status and withholding allowances claimed on Form W-4.

Employees may claim fewer withholding allowances than they are entitled to claim. They may do this to ensure that they have enough withholding or to offset other sources of taxable income that aren't subject to withholding.

See Pub. 505 for more information about completing Form W-4. Along with Form W-4, you may wish to order Pub. 505 for use by your employees.

Don't accept any withholding or estimated tax payments from your employees in addition to withholding based on their Form W-4. If an employee wants additional withholding, he or she should submit a new Form W-4 and, if necessary, pay estimated tax by filing Form 1040-ES or by using EFTPS to make estimated tax payments.

Exemption from federal income tax withholding. Generally, an employee may claim exemption from federal income tax withholding because he or she had no federal income tax liability last year and expects none this year. See the Form W-4 instructions for more information. However, the wages are still subject to social security and Medicare taxes.

A Form W-4 claiming exemption from withholding is effective when it is filed with the employer and only for that calendar year. To continue to be exempt from withholding in the next calendar year, an employee must give you a new Form W-4 by February 15. If the employee doesn't give you a new Form W-4 by February 15, withhold tax based on the last valid Form W-4 you have for the employee that didn't claim an exemption from withholding or, if one doesn't exist, withhold as if he or she is single with zero withholding allowances. If the employee provides a new Form W-4 claiming an exemption from withholding on February 16 or later, you may apply the exemption to future wages, but don't refund taxes withheld while the exempt status wasn't in place.

Withholding income taxes on the wages of nonresident alien employees. In general, you must withhold federal income taxes on the wages of nonresident alien employees. However, see Pub. 515 for exceptions to this general rule. Also see *Compensation paid to H-2A visa workers* in section 3.

Withholding adjustment for nonresident alien employees. A special procedure applies for figuring the amount of income tax to withhold from wages of nonresident alien employees performing services within the United States for wages paid in 2016. This procedure requires a special chart to be used with the withholding tables to determine the amount to withhold from the wages of the nonresident alien employee. See *Withholding adjustment for nonresident alien employees* in section 9 of Pub. 15.

Nonresident alien employee's Form W-4. When completing Forms W-4, nonresident aliens are required to:

- Not claim exemption from income tax withholding;

- Request withholding as if they are single, regardless of their actual marital status;

- Claim only one allowance (if the nonresident alien is a resident of Canada, Mexico, or Korea, or student or business apprentice from India, he or she may claim more than one allowance); and

- Write "Nonresident Alien" or "NRA" above the dotted line on line 6 of Form W-4.

If you maintain an electronic Form W-4 system, you should provide a field for nonresident alien employees to enter nonresident alien status instead of writing "Nonresident Alien" or "NRA" above the dotted line on line 6.

 A nonresident alien employee may request additional withholding at his or her option for other purposes, although such additions shouldn't be necessary for withholding to cover federal income tax liability related to employment.

Form 8233. If a nonresident alien employee claims a tax treaty exemption from withholding, the employee must submit Form 8233 with respect to the income exempt under the treaty, instead of Form W-4. See Pub. 515 for details.

IRS review of requested Forms W-4. When requested by the IRS, you must make original Forms W-4 available for inspection by an IRS employee. You may also be directed to send certain Forms W-4 to the IRS. You may receive a notice from the IRS requiring you to submit a copy of Form W-4 for one or more of your named employees. Send the requested copy or copies of Form W-4 to the IRS at the address provided and in the manner directed by the notice. The IRS may also require you to submit copies of Form W-4 to the IRS as directed by a revenue procedure or notice published in the Internal Revenue Bulletin. When we refer to Form W-4, the same rules apply to Formulario W-4(SP), its Spanish translation.

After submitting a copy of the requested Form W-4 to the IRS, continue to withhold federal income tax based on that Form W-4 if it is valid (see *Invalid Forms W-4*, later in this section). However, if the IRS later notifies you in writing that the employee isn't entitled to claim a complete exemption from withholding or more than the maximum number of withholding allowances specified by the IRS in the written notice, withhold federal income tax based on the effective date, marital status, and maximum number of withholding allowances specified in the notice (commonly referred to as a "lock-in letter").

Initial lock-in letter. The IRS uses information reported on Form W-2 to identify employees with withholding compliance problems. In some cases, where a serious under-withholding problem is found to exist for a particular employee, the IRS may issue a lock-in letter to the employer specifying the maximum number of withholding allowances and marital status permitted for a specific employee. You will also receive a copy for the employee that identifies the maximum number of withholding allowances permitted and the process by which the employee can provide additional information to the IRS for purposes of determining the appropriate number of withholding allowances. If the employee is employed by you as of the date of the notice, you must furnish the employee copy to the employee within 10 business days of receipt. You may follow any reasonable business practice to furnish the employee copy to the employee.

Implementation of lock-in letter. When you receive the notice specifying the maximum number of withholding allowances and marital status permitted, you may not withhold immediately on the basis of the notice. You must begin withholding tax on the basis of the notice for any wages paid after the date specified in the notice. The delay between your receipt of the notice and the date to begin the withholding on the basis of the notice permits the employee to contact the IRS.

Seasonal employees and employees not currently performing services. If you receive a notice for an employee who isn't currently performing services for you, you are still required to furnish the employee copy to the employee and withhold based on the notice if any of the following apply.

- You are paying wages for the employee's prior services and the wages are subject to income tax withholding on or after the date specified in the notice.

- You reasonably expect the employee to resume services within 12 months of the date of the notice.

- The employee is on a leave of absence that doesn't exceed 12 months or the employee has a right to re-employment after the leave of absence.

Termination and re-hire of employees. If you are required to furnish and withhold based on the notice and the employment relationship is terminated after the date of the notice, you must continue to withhold based on the notice if you continue to pay any wages subject to income tax withholding. You must also withhold based on the notice or modification notice (explained next) if the employee resumes the employment relationship with you within 12 months after the termination of the employment relationship.

Modification notice. After issuing the notice specifying the maximum number of withholding allowances and marital status permitted, the IRS may issue a subsequent notice (modification notice) that modifies the original notice. The modification notice may change the marital status and/or the number of withholding allowances permitted. You must withhold federal income tax based on the effective date specified in the modification notice.

New Form W-4 after IRS notice. After the IRS issues a notice or modification notice, if the employee provides you with a new Form W-4 claiming complete exemption from withholding or claims a marital status, a number of withholding allowances, and any additional withholding that results in less withholding than would result under the IRS notice or modification notice, you must disregard the new Form W-4. You are required to withhold on the basis of the notice or modification notice unless the IRS subsequently notifies you to withhold based on the new Form W-4. If the employee wants to put a new Form W-4 into effect that results in less withholding than required, the employee must contact the IRS.

If, after you receive an IRS notice or modification notice, your employee provides you with a new Form W-4 that doesn't claim exemption from federal income tax withholding and claims a marital status, a number of withholding allowances, and any additional withholding that results in more withholding than would result under the notice or modification notice, you must withhold tax on the basis of that new Form W-4. Otherwise, disregard any subsequent Forms W-4 provided by the employee and withhold based on the IRS notice or modification notice.

Substitute Forms W-4. You are encouraged to have your employees use the official version of Form W-4 to claim withholding allowances or exemption from withholding.

You may use a substitute version of Form W-4 to meet your business needs. However, your substitute Form W-4 must contain language that is identical to the official Form W-4 and your form must meet all current IRS rules for substitute forms. At the time that you provide your substitute form to the employee, you must provide him or her with all tables, instructions, and worksheets from the current Form W-4.

You can't accept a substitute Form W-4 developed by an employee, and the employee submitting such form will be treated as failing to furnish a Form W-4. However, continue to use any valid Forms W-4 developed by your employees that you accepted before October 11, 2007.

Invalid Forms W-4. Any unauthorized change or addition to Form W-4 makes it invalid. This includes taking out any language by which the employee certifies that the form is correct. A Form W-4 is also invalid if, by the date an employee gives it to you, he or she indicates in any way that it is false. An employee who submits a false Form W-4 may be subject to a $500 penalty. You may treat a Form W-4 as invalid if the employee wrote "exempt" on line 7 and also entered a number on line 5 or an amount on line 6.

When you get an invalid Form W-4, don't use it to figure federal income tax withholding. Tell the employee that it is invalid and ask for another one. If the employee doesn't give you a valid one, withhold tax as if the employee is single with zero withholding allowances. However, if you have an earlier Form W-4 for this worker that is valid, withhold as you did before.

For additional information about these rules, see Treasury Decision 9337, 2007-35 I.R.B. 455, available at *www.irs.gov/irb/2007-35_IRB/ar10.html*.

Amounts exempt from levy on wages, salary, and other income. If you receive a Notice of Levy on Wages, Salary, and Other Income—Forms 668-W(ACS), 668-W(c)(DO), or 668-W(ICS), you must withhold amounts as described in the instructions for these forms. Pub. 1494 has tables to figure the amount exempt from levy. If a levy issued in a prior year is still in effect and the taxpayer submits a new Statement of Exemptions and Filing Status, use the current year Pub. 1494 to compute the exempt amount.

How To Figure Federal Income Tax Withholding

There are several ways to figure federal income tax withholding.

- Wage bracket tables. See section 13 for directions on how to use the tables.

- Percentage method. See section 13 for directions on how to use the percentage method.

- Alternative formula tables for percentage method withholding. See Pub. 15-A.

- Wage bracket percentage method withholding tables. See Pub. 15-A.

- Other alternative methods. See Pub. 15-A.

Employers with automated payroll systems will find the two alternative formula tables and the two alternative wage bracket percentage method tables in Pub. 15-A useful.

If an employee wants additional federal tax withheld, have the employee show the extra amount on Form W-4.

Supplemental wages. Supplemental wages are wage payments to an employee that aren't regular wages. They include, but aren't limited to, bonuses, commissions, overtime pay, accumulated sick leave, severance pay, awards, prizes, back pay and retroactive pay increases for current employees, and payments for nondeductible moving expenses. Other payments subject to the supplemental wage rules include taxable fringe benefits and expense allowances paid under a nonaccountable plan.

If you pay supplemental wages with regular wages but don't specify the amount of each, withhold federal income tax as if the total was a single payment for a regular payroll period.

If you pay supplemental wages separately (or combine them in a single payment and specify the amount of each), the federal income tax withholding method depends partly on whether you withhold federal income tax from your employee's regular wages.

1. If you withheld federal income tax from an employee's regular wages in the current or immediately preceding calendar year, you can use one of the following methods for the supplemental wages.

    a. Withhold a flat 25% (no other percentage allowed).

    b. If the supplemental wages are paid concurrently with regular wages, add the supplemental wages to the concurrently paid regular wages. If there are no concurrently paid regular wages, add the supplemental wages to alternatively, either the regular wages paid or to be paid for the current payroll period or the regular wages paid for the preceding payroll period. Figure the income tax withholding as if the total of the regular wages and supplemental wages is a single payment. Subtract the tax withheld from the regular wages. Withhold the remaining tax from the supplemental wages. If there were other payments of supplemental wages paid during the payroll period made before the current payment of supplemental wages, aggregate all the payments of supplemental wages paid during the payroll period with the regular wages paid during the payroll period, calculate the tax on the total, subtract the tax already withheld from the regular wages and previous supplemental wage payments, and withhold the remaining tax from the current payment of supplemental wages.

2. If you didn't withhold federal income tax from the employee's regular wages in the current or immediately preceding calendar year, use method 1-b above. This would occur, for example, when the value of the employee's withholding allowances claimed on Form W-4 is more than the wages.

 *Separate rules apply to any supplemental wages exceeding $1 million that you pay to an individual during the year. See section 7 in Pub. 15 for details.*

Regardless of the method that you use to withhold federal income tax on supplemental wages, they are generally subject to social security, Medicare, and FUTA taxes.

---

6. Required Notice to Employees About Earned Income Credit (EIC)

You must notify employees who have no federal income tax withheld that they may be able to claim a tax refund because of the EIC. Although you don't have to notify employees who claim exemption from withholding on Form W-4 about the EIC, you are encouraged to notify any employees whose wages for 2015 were less than $47,747 ($53,267 if married filing jointly) that they may be eligible to claim the credit for 2015. This is because eligible employees may get a refund of the amount of EIC that is more than the tax that they owe.

You will meet the notification requirement if you issue to the employee Form W-2 with the EIC notice on the back of Copy B, or a substitute Form W-2 with the same statement. You may also meet the requirement by providing Notice 797, Possible Federal Tax Refund Due to the Earned Income Credit (EIC), or your own statement that contains the same wording.

If a substitute Form W-2 is given to the employee on time but doesn't have the required statement, you must notify the employee within 1 week of the date that the substitute Form W-2 is given. If Form W-2 is required but isn't given on time, you must give the employee Notice 797 or your written statement by the date that Form W-2 is required to be given. If Form W-2 isn't required, you must notify the employee by February 8, 2016.

7. Depositing Taxes

Generally, you must deposit both the employer and employee shares of social security and Medicare taxes and federal income tax withheld. You must use EFT to make all federal tax deposits. See *How To Deposit*, later in this section.

 The credit against employment taxes for COBRA premium assistance payments is treated as a deposit of taxes on the first day of your return period. For more information, see COBRA premium assistance credit *under* Introduction.

Payment with return. You may make payments with Forms 943 or 945 instead of depositing if one of the following applies.

- You report less than a $2,500 tax liability for the year (Form 943, line 11; Form 945, line 3) and you pay in full with a return that is filed on time. However, if you are unsure that you will report less than $2,500, deposit under the rules explained in this section so that you won't be subject to a failure-to-deposit (FTD) penalty.

- You are a monthly schedule depositor and make a payment in accordance with the *Accuracy of Deposits Rule* discussed later in this section. This payment may be $2,500 or more.

 Only monthly schedule depositors, defined later, are allowed to make an Accuracy of Deposits Rule payment with the return. Semiweekly schedule depositors must timely deposit the amount. See Accuracy of Deposits Rule *and* How To Deposit, *later in this section.*

When To Deposit

 If you employ both farm and nonfarm workers, don't combine the taxes reportable on Forms 941 or 944 with Form 943 to decide whether to make a deposit. See Employers of Both Farm and Nonfarm Workers, *later in this section.*

The rules for determining when to deposit Form 943 taxes are discussed below. See section 10 for the separate rules that apply to FUTA tax. Under these rules, you are classified as either a monthly schedule depositor or a semiweekly schedule depositor.

The terms "monthly schedule depositor" and "semiweekly schedule depositor" don't refer to how often your business pays its employees or how often you are required to make deposits. The terms identify which set of rules you must follow when you incur a tax liability (for example, when you have a payday).

The deposit schedule that you must use for a calendar year is determined from the tax liability reported on your

Form 943, line 11, for the lookback period, discussed next.

- If you reported $50,000 or less of Form 943 taxes for the lookback period, you are a monthly schedule depositor.

- If you reported more than $50,000 of Form 943 taxes for the lookback period, you are a semiweekly schedule depositor.

Lookback period. The lookback period is the second calendar year preceding the current calendar year. For example, the lookback period for 2016 is 2014.

Example of deposit schedule based on lookback period. Rose Co. reported taxes on Form 943 as follows.

    2014 — $48,000

    2015 — $60,000

Rose Co. is a monthly schedule depositor for 2016 because its taxes for the lookback period ($48,000 for calendar year 2014) weren't more than $50,000. However, for 2017, Rose Co. is a semiweekly schedule depositor because the total taxes before adjustment for its lookback period ($60,000 for calendar year 2015) exceeded $50,000.

Adjustments to lookback period taxes. To determine your taxes for the lookback period, use only the tax that you reported on the original return (Form 943, line 11). Don't include adjustments shown on Form 943-X.

Example of adjustments. An employer originally reported total tax of $45,000 for the lookback period in 2014. The employer discovered during March 2016 that the tax reported for the lookback period was understated by $10,000 and corrected this error by filing Form 943-X. The total tax reported in the lookback period is still $45,000. The $10,000 adjustment is also not treated as part of the 2016 taxes.

Deposit period. The term "deposit period" refers to the period during which tax liabilities are accumulated for each required deposit due date. For monthly schedule depositors, the deposit period is a calendar month. The deposit periods for semiweekly schedule depositors are Wednesday through Friday and Saturday through Tuesday.

Monthly Deposit Schedule

If the tax liability reported on Form 943, line 11, for the lookback period is $50,000 or less, you are a monthly schedule depositor for the current year. You must deposit Form 943 taxes on payments made during a calendar month by the 15th day of the following month.

Monthly schedule example. Red Co. is a seasonal employer and a monthly schedule depositor. It pays wages each Friday. It paid wages during May 2016, but didn't pay any wages during June. Red Co. must deposit the combined tax liabilities for the May paydays by June 15. Red Co. doesn't have a deposit requirement for June (that is, due by July 15, 2016) because no wages were paid in June; therefore, it didn't have a tax liability for June.

New employers. For agricultural employers, your tax liability for any year in the lookback period before the date you started or acquired your business is considered to be zero. Therefore, you are a monthly schedule depositor for the first and second calendar years of your agricultural business (but see the *$100,000 Next-Day Deposit Rule*, later in this section).

Semiweekly Deposit Schedule

You are a semiweekly schedule depositor for a calendar year if the tax liability on Form 943, line 11, during your lookback period was more than $50,000. Under the semiweekly deposit schedule, deposit Form 943 taxes for payments made on Wednesday, Thursday, and/or Friday by the following Wednesday. Deposit amounts accumulated for payments made on Saturday, Sunday, Monday, and/or Tuesday by the following Friday.

Semiweekly depositors aren't required to deposit twice a week if their payments were in the same semiweekly period unless the *$100,000 Next-Day Deposit Rule* (discussed later in this section) applies. For example, if you made a payment on both Wednesday and Friday and incurred taxes of $10,000 for each pay date, deposit the $20,000 by the following Wednesday. If you made no additional payments on Saturday through Tuesday, no deposit is due on Friday.

 Semiweekly schedule depositors must complete Form 943-A, Agricultural Employer's Record of Federal Tax Liability, and submit it with Form 943.

Semiweekly Deposit Schedule

IF the payday falls on a...	THEN deposit taxes by the following...
Wednesday, Thursday, and/or Friday	Wednesday
Saturday, Sunday, Monday, and/or Tuesday	Friday

Semiweekly schedule example. Green, Inc., is a semiweekly schedule depositor and pays wages once each month on the last Friday of the month. Green, Inc., will deposit only once a month, but the deposit will be made under the semiweekly deposit schedule as follows. Green, Inc.'s tax liability for the April 29, 2016 (Friday), wage payment must be deposited by May 4, 2016 (Wednesday).

Semiweekly deposit period spanning two quarters. If you have more than one pay date during a semiweekly period and the pay dates fall in different calendar quarters, you will need to make separate deposits for the separate liabilities. For example, if you have a pay date on Thursday, March 31, 2016 (first quarter), and another pay date on Friday, April 1, 2016 (second quarter), two separate deposits will be required even though the pay dates fall within the same semiweekly period. Both deposits will be due Wednesday, April 6, 2016 (3 business days from the end of the semiweekly deposit period).

Deposits on Business Days Only

If a deposit is required to be made on a day that isn't a business day, the deposit is considered timely if it is made by the close of the next business day. A business day is any day other than a Saturday, Sunday, or legal holiday. For example, if a deposit is required to be made on Friday and Friday is a legal holiday, the deposit is considered timely if it is made by the following Monday (if Monday is a business day).

Semiweekly schedule depositors will always have 3 business days to make a deposit. That is, if any of the 3 weekdays after the end of a semiweekly period is a legal holiday, you will have an additional day for each day that is a legal holiday to make the deposit. For example, if a semiweekly schedule depositor accumulated taxes on Friday and the following Monday is a legal holiday, the deposit normally due on Wednesday may be made on Thursday (this allows 3 business days to make the deposit).

Legal holiday. The term "legal holiday" means any legal holiday in the District of Columbia. Legal holidays for 2016 are listed below.

- January 1—New Year's Day
- January 18—Birthday of Martin Luther King, Jr.
- February 15—Washington's Birthday
- April 15—District of Columbia Emancipation Day (observed)
- May 30—Memorial Day
- July 4—Independence Day
- September 5—Labor Day
- October 10—Columbus Day
- November 11—Veterans' Day
- November 24—Thanksgiving Day
- December 26—Christmas Day (observed)

$100,000 Next-Day Deposit Rule

If you accumulate $100,000 or more of Form 943 taxes (that is, taxes reported on Form 943, line 11) on any day during a deposit period, you must deposit the tax by the close of the next business day, whether you are a monthly or a semiweekly schedule depositor.

For purposes of the $100,000 rule, don't continue accumulating a tax liability after the end of a deposit period.

For example, if a semiweekly schedule depositor has accumulated a liability of $95,000 on a Tuesday (of a Saturday-through-Tuesday deposit period) and accumulated a $10,000 liability on Wednesday, the $100,000 next-day deposit rule doesn't apply because the $10,000 is accumulated in the next deposit period. Thus, $95,000 must be deposited by Friday and $10,000 must be deposited by the following Wednesday.

However, once you accumulate at least $100,000 in a deposit period, stop accumulating at the end of that day and begin to accumulate anew on the next day. For example, Fir Co. is a semiweekly schedule depositor. On Monday, Fir Co. accumulates taxes of $110,000 and must deposit this amount on Tuesday, the next business day. On Tuesday, Fir Co. accumulates additional taxes of $30,000. Because the $30,000 isn't added to the previous $110,000 and is less than $100,000, Fir Co. doesn't have to deposit the $30,000 until Friday (following the semiweekly deposit schedule).

 If you are a monthly schedule depositor and you accumulate a $100,000 tax liability on any day, you become a semiweekly schedule depositor on the next day and remain so for at least the rest of the calendar year and for the following calendar year.

Example of the $100,000 next-day deposit rule. Elm, Inc., started its business on May 1, 2016. Because Elm, Inc., is a new employer, the taxes for its lookback period are considered to be zero; therefore, Elm, Inc., is a monthly schedule depositor. On May 4, Elm, Inc., paid wages for the first time and accumulated taxes of $50,000. On May 6 (Friday), Elm, Inc., paid wages and accumulated taxes of $60,000, for a total of $110,000. Because Elm, Inc., accumulated $110,000 on May 6, it must deposit $110,000 by May 9 (Monday), the next business day. Elm, Inc., became a semiweekly schedule depositor on May 7. It will be a semiweekly schedule depositor for the remainder of 2016 and for 2017.

Accuracy of Deposits Rule

You are required to deposit 100% of your tax liability on or before the deposit due date. However, penalties won't be applied for depositing less than 100% if both of the following conditions are met.

1. Any deposit shortfall doesn't exceed the greater of $100 or 2% of the amount of taxes otherwise required to be deposited.

2. The deposit shortfall is paid or deposited by the shortfall makeup date as described below.

Makeup Date for Deposit Shortfall:

- **Monthly Schedule Depositor**—Deposit the shortfall or pay it with your return by the due date of your Form 943. You may pay the shortfall with your Form 943 even if the amount is $2,500 or more.

- **Semiweekly Schedule Depositor**—Deposit by the earlier of (a) the first Wednesday or Friday (whichever comes first) that falls on or after the 15th of the month following the month in which the shortfall occurred, or (b) the due date for Form 943. For example, if a semiweekly schedule depositor has a deposit shortfall during February 2016, the shortfall makeup date is March 16, 2016 (Wednesday).

How To Deposit

You must deposit employment taxes by EFT. See *Payment with return*, earlier in this section, for exceptions explaining when taxes may be paid with the tax return instead of being deposited.

Electronic deposit requirement. You must use EFT to make all federal tax deposits (such as deposits of employment tax, excise tax, and corporate income tax). Generally, an EFT is made using EFTPS. If you don't want to use EFTPS, you can arrange for your tax professional, financial institution, payroll service, or other trusted third-party to make electronic deposits on your behalf.

EFTPS is a free service provided by the Department of Treasury. To get more information or to enroll in EFTPS, call 1-800-555-4477 (business), 1-800-316-6541 (individual), or 1-800-733-4829 (TDD). You can also visit the EFTPS website at *www.eftps.gov*. Additional information about EFTPS is also available in Pub. 966.

New employers that have a federal tax obligation will be pre-enrolled in EFTPS. Call the toll-free number located in your EIN Package to activate your enrollment and begin making your tax deposit payments. See *When you receive your EIN* in section 1 for more information.

Deposit record. For your records, an EFT Trace Number will be provided with each successful payment. The number can be used as a receipt or to trace the payment.

Depositing on time. For deposits made by EFTPS to be on time, you must submit the deposit by 8 p.m. Eastern time the day before the date a deposit is due. If you use a third-party to make a deposit on your behalf, they may have different cutoff times.

Same-day wire payment option. If you fail to submit a deposit transaction on EFTPS by 8 p.m. Eastern time the day before the date a deposit is due, you can still make your deposit on time by using the Federal Tax Collection Service (FTCS). To use the same-day wire payment method, you will need to make arrangements with your financial institution ahead of time. Please check with your financial institution regarding availability, deadlines, and costs. Your financial institution may charge you a fee for payments made this way. To learn more about the information you will need to provide your financial institution to make a same-day wire payment, visit the IRS website at *www.irs.gov/payments* and click on *Same-day wire*.

Deposit Penalties

Penalties may apply if you don't make required deposits on time or if you make deposits for less than the required amount. The penalties don't apply if any failure to make a proper and timely deposit was due to reasonable cause and not to willful neglect. If you receive a penalty notice, you can provide an explanation of why you believe reasonable cause exists. IRS may also waive deposit penalties if you inadvertently fail to deposit in the first quarter that a deposit is due, or the first quarter during which your frequency of deposits changed, if you timely filed your employment tax return.

For amounts not properly deposited or not deposited on time, the penalty rates are shown next.

Penalty	Charged for...
2%	Deposits made 1 to 5 days late.
5%	Deposits made 6 to 15 days late.
10%	Deposits made 16 or more days late. Also applies to amounts paid within 10 days of the date of the first notice the IRS sent asking for the tax due.
10%	Amounts (that should have been deposited) paid directly to the IRS or paid with your tax return. See *Payment with return*, earlier in this section, for exceptions.
15%	Amounts still unpaid more than 10 days after the date of the first notice that the IRS sent asking for the tax due or the day on which you received notice and demand for immediate payment, whichever is earlier.

Late deposit penalty amounts are determined using calendar days, starting from the due date of the liability.

Order in which deposits are applied. Deposits generally are applied to the most recent tax liability within the year. If you receive an FTD penalty notice, you may designate how your deposits are to be applied in order to minimize the amount of the penalty, if you do so within 90 days of the date of the notice. Follow the instructions on the penalty notice that you received. For examples on how the IRS will apply deposits and more information on designating deposits, see Revenue Procedure 2001-58. You can find Revenue Procedure 2001-58 on page 579 of Internal Revenue Bulletin 2001-50 at *www.irs.gov/pub/irs-irbs/irb01-50.pdf*.

Example. Cedar, Inc., is required to make a deposit of $1,000 on May 15 and $1,500 on June 15. It doesn't make the deposit on May 15. On June 15, Cedar, Inc., deposits $2,000. Under the deposits rule, which applies deposits to the most recent tax liability, $1,500 of the deposit is applied to the June 15 deposit and the remaining $500 is applied to the May deposit. Accordingly, $500 of the May 15 liability remains undeposited. The penalty on this under-deposit will apply as explained above.

Trust fund recovery penalty. If federal income, social security, or Medicare taxes that must be withheld aren't withheld or aren't deposited or paid to the United States Treasury, the trust fund recovery penalty may apply. The penalty is the full amount of the unpaid trust fund tax. This penalty may apply to you if these unpaid taxes can't be immediately collected from the employer or business.

The trust fund recovery penalty may be imposed on all persons who are determined by the IRS to be responsible for collecting, accounting for, or paying over these taxes, and who acted willfully in not doing so.

A **responsible person** can be an officer or employee of a corporation, a partner or employee of a partnership, an accountant, a volunteer director/trustee, or an employee of a sole proprietorship. A responsible person also may include one who signs checks for the business or otherwise has authority to cause the spending of business funds.

Willfully means voluntarily, consciously, and intentionally. A responsible person acts willfully if the person knows that the required actions of collecting, accounting for, or paying over trust fund taxes aren't taking place, or recklessly disregards obvious and known risks to the government's right to receive trust fund taxes.

"Average" FTD penalty. IRS may assess an "averaged" FTD penalty of 2% to 10% if you are a monthly schedule depositor and didn't properly complete Form 943, line 17, when your tax liability shown on Form 943, line 11, was $2,500 or more. IRS may also assess this penalty of 2% to 10% if you are a semiweekly schedule depositor and your tax liability shown on Form 943, line 11, was $2,500 or more and you did any of the following.

- Completed Form 943, line 17, instead of Form 943-A.

- Failed to attach a properly completed Form 943-A.

- Completed Form 943-A incorrectly, for example, by entering tax deposits instead of tax liabilities in the numbered spaces.

The IRS figures the penalty by allocating your tax liability on Form 943, line 11, equally throughout the tax period. Your deposits and payments may not be counted as timely because the IRS doesn't know the actual dates of your tax liabilities.

You can avoid the penalty by reviewing your return before filing it. Follow these steps before filing your Form 943.

- If you are a monthly schedule depositor, report your tax liabilities (not your deposits) in the monthly entry spaces on Form 943, line 17.

- If you are a semiweekly schedule depositor, report your tax liabilities (not your deposits) on Form 943-A in the lines that represent the dates you paid your employees.

- Verify that your total liability shown on Form 943, line 17, or Form 943-A, line M, equals your tax liability shown on Form 943, line 11.

- Don't show negative amounts on Form 943, line 17, or Form 943-A.

- For prior period errors don't adjust your tax liabilities reported on Form 943, line 17, or on Form 943-A.

Employers of Both Farm and Nonfarm Workers

If you employ both farm and nonfarm workers, you must treat employment taxes for the farmworkers (Form 943 taxes) separately from employment taxes for the nonfarm workers (Form 941 and 944 taxes). Form 943 taxes and Form 941/944 taxes aren't combined for purposes of applying any of the deposit schedule rules.

If a deposit is due, deposit the Form 941/944 taxes and the Form 943 taxes by making separate deposits. For example, if you are a monthly schedule depositor for both Forms 941/944 and 943 taxes and your tax liability at the end of May is $1,500, reportable on Form 941/944 and $1,200 reportable on Form 943, deposit both amounts by June 15. Use one transaction to deposit the $1,500 of Form 941/944 taxes and another transaction to deposit the $1,200 of Form 943 taxes.

8. Form 943

You must file Form 943 for each calendar year beginning with the first year that you pay $2,500 or more for farmwork or you employ a farmworker who meets the $150 test explained in section 4. Don't report these wages on Form 941 or Form 944.

Household employees. If you file Form 943 and pay wages to household workers, you may include the wages and taxes of these workers on Form 943. If you choose not to report these wages and taxes on Form 943, report the wages of these workers separately on Schedule H (Form 1040). You must have an EIN to file Schedule H (Form 1040). See section 1 for details. If you report the wages on Form 943, include the taxes when you figure deposit requirements or make deposits. If you include household employee wages and taxes on Schedule H (Form 1040), don't include the household employee taxes when you figure deposit requirements or make Form 943 deposits. See Pub. 926 for more information about household workers.

If household employee wages and taxes are included on Form 943, you must also include FUTA tax for the employees on Form 940. See section 10 for more information.

Penalties. For each month or part of a month that a return isn't filed when required (disregarding any extensions of the filing deadline), there is a failure-to-file (FTF) penalty of 5% of the unpaid tax due with that return. The maximum penalty is 25% of the tax due. Also, for each month or part of a month that the tax is paid late (disregarding any extensions of the payment deadline), there is a failure-to-pay (FTP) penalty of 0.5% per month of the amount of tax. For individual filers only, the FTP penalty is reduced from 0.5% per month to 0.25% per month if an installment agreement is in effect. You must have filed your return on or before the due date of the return to qualify for the reduced penalty. The maximum amount of the FTP penalty is also 25% of the tax due. If both penalties apply in any month, the FTF penalty is reduced by the amount of the FTP penalty. The penalties won't be charged if you have reasonable cause for failing to file or pay. If you receive a penalty notice, you can provide an explanation of why you believe reasonable cause exists.

Note. In addition to any penalties, interest accrues from the due date of the tax on any unpaid balance.

If federal income, social security, or Medicare taxes that must be withheld aren't withheld or aren't paid, you may be personally liable for the trust fund recovery penalty. See _Trust fund recovery penalty_ in section 7.

Use of a third-party payer, such as a payroll service provider or reporting agent, doesn't relieve an employer of the responsibility to ensure that tax returns are filed and all taxes are paid or deposited correctly and on time.

9. Reporting Adjustments on Form 943

There are two types of adjustments: current year adjustments and prior year adjustments to correct errors. See the Instructions for Form 943 and the Instructions for Form 943-X for more information on how to report these adjustments.

Current Year Adjustments

In certain cases, amounts reported as social security and Medicare taxes on Form 943, lines 3, 5, and 7, must be adjusted to arrive at your correct tax liability. The most common situation involves differences in cents totals due to rounding. Other situations when current year adjustments may be necessary include third-party sick pay, group-term life insurance for former employees, and the uncollected employee share of social security and Medicare taxes on tips. Current year adjustments are reported on Form 943, line 10. See Pub. 15 for more information on these adjustments.

If you withhold an incorrect amount of federal income tax or Additional Medicare Tax from an employee, you may adjust the amount withheld in later pay periods during the **same year** to compensate for the error.

Prior Year Adjustments

If you discover an error on a previously filed Form 943, make the correction using Form 943-X. File a separate Form 943-X for each prior year you are correcting. File Form 943-X separately. Don't attach Form 943-X to your current period Form 943. You must explain your error on Form 943-X, indicate when the error was discovered, and provide the applicable certifications.

When you discover that you underreported tax on a previously filed return, you must file Form 943-X no later than the due date of the return for the period during which you discovered the error. Pay the amount you owe by the time you file. For example, you discover on June 10,

2016, that you underreported $10,000 of social security and Medicare wages on your 2015 Form 943. You owe $1,530 on the 2015 Form 943. To qualify for an interest-free adjustment, you must file Form 943-X by January 31, 2017, and pay $1,530 by the time you file. For more information, see the Instructions for Form 943-X or visit IRS.gov and enter "correcting employment taxes" in the search box.

TIP *See Revenue Ruling 2009-39, 2009-52 I.R.B. 951, for examples of how the interest-free adjustment and claim for refund rules apply in 10 different situations. You can find Revenue Ruling 2009-39, at www.irs.gov/irb/2009-52_IRB/ar14.html.*

Form 843. Don't use Form 843 to request a refund or abatement of overreported social security or Medicare taxes. Instead, request your refund or abatement of taxes on Form 943-X. However, use Form 843 when requesting a refund or abatement of assessed interest or penalties.

Federal income tax and Additional Medicare Tax withholding adjustments. You can't adjust amounts reported as income tax or Additional Medicare Tax withheld in a prior calendar year, even if you withheld the wrong amount, unless it is to correct an administrative error or section 3509 applies. An administrative error occurs if the amount you entered on Form 943 is not the amount that you actually withheld. Examples include mathematical or transposition errors. In these cases, you should adjust the return to show the amount actually withheld.

If a prior year error was a nonadministrative error, you may correct only the **wages** subject to Additional Medicare Tax withholding.

Social security and Medicare tax adjustments. Correct prior year social security and Medicare tax errors by making an adjustment on Form 943-X.

If you withheld no tax or less than the correct amount, you may correct the mistake by withholding the tax from a later payment to the same employee.

If you withheld employee tax when no tax is due or if you withheld more than the correct amount, you must repay or reimburse the employee.

Collecting underwithheld taxes from employees. If you withheld no federal income, social security, or Medicare taxes or less than the correct amount from an employee's wages, you can make it up from future pay to that employee. But you are the one who owes the underpayment. Reimbursement is a matter for settlement between you and the employee. Underwithheld federal income tax and Additional Medicare Tax must be recovered from the employee on or before the last day of the calendar year.

Refunding amounts incorrectly withheld from employees. If you withheld more than the correct amount of income, social security, or Medicare taxes from wages paid, repay or reimburse the employee the excess. Any excess income tax or Additional Medicare Tax withholding must be repaid or reimbursed to the employee before the end of the calendar year in which it was withheld. Keep in your records the employee's written receipt showing the date and amount of the repayment or record of reimbursement. If you didn't repay or reimburse the employee, you must report and pay each excess amount when you file Form 943 for the year in which you withheld too much tax.

Filing corrections to Forms W-2 and W-3. When adjustments are made to correct social security and Medicare taxes because of a change in the wage totals reported for a previous year, you also may need to file Forms W-2c and Form W-3c. Forms W-2c may be created and submitted to SSA over the Internet. For more information, visit SSA's Employer W-2 Filing Instructions & Information website at www.socialsecurity.gov/employer.

For additional information about the procedure for adjusting employment taxes, see the Instructions for Form 943-X or visit IRS.gov and enter "correcting employment taxes" in the search box. Also see Treasury Decision 9405, 2008-32 I.R.B. 293, available at www.irs.gov/irb/2008-32_IRB/ar13.html.

Note. Continue to make current period adjustments for fractions of cents, sick pay, tips, and group-term life insurance on your Form 943.

10. Federal Unemployment (FUTA) Tax

The Federal Unemployment Tax Act (FUTA), with state unemployment systems, provides for payments of unemployment compensation to workers who have lost their jobs. Most employers pay both a federal and a state unemployment tax. For a list of state unemployment agencies, visit the U.S. Department of Labor's website at www.workforcesecurity.doleta.gov/unemploy/agencies.asp. Only the employer pays FUTA tax; it isn't withheld from the employees' wages. For more information, see the Instructions for Form 940.

For 2016, you must file Form 940, if you:

- Paid cash wages of $20,000 or more to farmworkers in any calendar quarter in 2015 or 2016, or

- Employed 10 or more farmworkers during at least some part of a day (whether or not at the same time) during any 20 or more different weeks in 2015 or 20 or more different weeks in 2016.

To determine whether you meet either test above, you must count wages paid to aliens admitted on a temporary basis to the United States to perform farmwork, also known as "H-2A" visa workers. However, wages paid to "H-2A" visa workers aren't subject to the FUTA tax.

Generally, farmworkers supplied by a **crew leader** are considered employees of the farm operator for purposes of the FUTA tax unless (a) the crew leader is registered under the Migrant and Seasonal Agricultural Worker Protection Act, or (b) substantially all of the workers supplied by the crew leader operate or maintain tractors, harvesting or crop-dusting machines, or other machines provided by the crew leader. Therefore, if (a) or (b) applies, the farmworkers are generally employees of the crew leader.

You must deposit FUTA tax by EFT. The deposit rules for FUTA tax are different from those for income, social security, and Medicare taxes. See *Deposit rules for FUTA tax*, later in this section.

FUTA tax rate. The FUTA tax rate is 6.0% for 2016. The tax applies to the first $7,000 you pay to each employee as wages during the year. The $7,000 is the federal wage base. Your state wage base may be different. Generally, you can take a credit against your FUTA tax for amounts you paid into state unemployment funds. The credit may be as much as 5.4% of wages subject to FUTA tax. If you are entitled to the maximum 5.4% credit, the FUTA tax rate after credit is 0.6%. You are entitled to the maximum credit if you paid your state unemployment taxes in full, on time, and on all the same wages as are subject to FUTA tax, and as long as the state isn't determined to be a credit reduction state. See the Instructions for Form 940 to determine the credit.

In some states, the wages subject to state unemployment tax are the same as the wages subject to FUTA tax. However, certain states exclude some types of wages from state unemployment tax, even though they are subject to FUTA tax (for example, wages paid to corporate officers, certain payments of sick pay by unions, and certain fringe benefits). In such a case, you may be required to deposit more than 0.6% FUTA tax on those wages. See the Instructions for Form 940 for further guidance.

Successor employer. If you have acquired a business from someone else, you may be able to claim a special credit as a successor employer. See the Instructions for Form 940.

Deposit rules for FUTA tax. Generally, deposit FUTA tax quarterly. To figure your FUTA tax, multiply .006 times the amount of wages paid to each employee during the quarter. This amount may need to be adjusted, however, depending on your entitlement to the credit for state unemployment contributions. See the Instructions for Form 940. When an employee's wages reach $7,000, don't figure any additional FUTA tax for that employee. If the FUTA tax for the quarter (plus any undeposited FUTA tax from prior quarters) is more than $500, deposit the FUTA tax by EFT as explained in section 7, by the last day of the month following the end of the quarter. If the amount is $500 or less, you don't have to deposit it, but you must add it to the amount of tax for the next quarter to determine whether a deposit is required for that quarter.

If your liability for the fourth quarter (plus any undeposited amount from any earlier quarter) is over $500, deposit the entire amount by the due date of Form 940 (January 31). If it is $500 or less, you can make a deposit, pay the tax with a major credit card, debit card, or pay the tax with a check or money order with your Form 940 by January 31. If you file Form 940 electronically, you can *e-file* and e-pay (EFW). For more information on paying your taxes with a credit or debit card or using EFW, visit the IRS website at *www.irs.gov/payments*.

Filing Form 940. File your 2015 Form 940 by February 1, 2016. If you make deposits on time in full payment of the tax due for the year, you may file Form 940 by February 10.

11. Reconciling Wage Reporting Forms

When there are discrepancies between amounts reported on Form 943 filed with the IRS and Forms W-2 and W-3 filed with the SSA, the IRS must contact you to resolve the discrepancies.

To help reduce discrepancies:

1. Report bonuses as wages and as social security and Medicare wages on Forms W-2 and 943;

2. Report social security and Medicare wages and taxes separately on Forms W-2, W-3, and 943;

3. Report social security taxes on Form W-2 in the box for social security tax withheld (box 4), not as social security wages;

4. Report Medicare taxes on Form W-2 in the box for Medicare tax withheld (box 6), not as Medicare wages;

5. Make sure that social security wages for each employee don't exceed the annual social security wage base; and

6. Don't report noncash wages that aren't subject to social security or Medicare taxes as social security or Medicare wages.

To reduce the discrepancies between amounts reported on Forms W-2, W-3, and 943:

1. Be sure that the amounts on Form W-3 are the total amounts from Forms W-2, excluding any amounts from Forms W-2 that were marked void, and

2. Reconcile Form W-3 with your Form 943 by comparing amounts reported for the following items.

- Federal income tax withholding, social security wages, and Medicare wages.

- Social security and Medicare taxes.

Amounts reported on Forms W-2, W-3, and 943 may not match for valid reasons. If they don't match, you should determine that the reasons are valid. Keep your reconciliation so that you will have a record of why amounts didn't match in case there are inquiries from the IRS or the SSA.

12. How Do Employment Taxes Apply to Farmwork?

Type of employment	Income Tax Withholding, Social Security, and Medicare (including Additional Medicare Tax when wages are paid in excess of $200,000)	Federal Unemployment Tax
Farm Employment Includes: 1. Cultivating soil; raising or harvesting any agricultural or horticultural commodity; the care of livestock, poultry, bees, fur-bearing animals, or wildlife. 2. Work on a farm if major farm duties are in management or maintenance, etc., of farm tools or equipment or salvaging timber, or clearing brush or other debris, left by hurricane. 3. Work in connection with the production and harvesting of turpentine and other oleoresinous products. 4. Cotton ginning. 5. Operating or maintenance of ditches, reservoirs, canals, or waterways used only for supplying or storing water for farming purposes and not owned or operated for profit. 6. Processing, packaging, etc., any commodity in its unmanufactured state if employed by farm operator who produced over half of commodity processed or by group of up to 20 unincorporated farm operators if they produced all the commodity. 7. Hatching poultry on a farm.* 8. Production or harvesting of maple syrup.	Taxable if $150 test or $2,500 test is met. See section 4.	Taxable if either test in section 10 is met.
Farm Employment Doesn't Include: 1. Handling or processing commodities after delivery to terminal market for commercial canning or freezing. 2. Operating or maintenance of ditches, canals, reservoirs or waterways not meeting tests in (5) above. 3. Processing, packaging, delivering, etc., any commodity in its unmanufactured state if group of farm operators don't meet the tests in (6) above. 4. Household employment.	Taxable under general employment rules. Farm rules don't apply.	Taxable under general FUTA rules. Farm rules don't apply.
Special Employment Situations: 1. Services not in the course of employer's trade or business on farm operated for profit (cash payments only). 2. Workers admitted under section 101(a)(15)(H)(ii)(a) of the Immigration and Nationality Act on a temporary basis to perform agricultural labor ("H-2A" workers). 3. Family employment.	Taxable if $150 test or $2,500 test is met (see section 4), unless performed by parent employed by child. Exempt. Exempt for employer's child under age 18, but counted for $150 test or $2,500 test. Taxable for spouse of employer.	Taxable only if $50 or more is paid in a quarter and employee works on 24 or more different days in current or prior quarter. Exempt. Exempt if services performed by employer's parent or spouse or by employer's child under age 21.

*Hatching poultry off the farm isn't considered farmwork for income tax withholding, social security, and Medicare. It is considered farmwork for federal unemployment tax.

13. Federal Income Tax Withholding Methods

There are several methods to figure federal income tax withholding for employees. The most common are the wage bracket method and the percentage method.

Wage Bracket Method

Under the wage bracket method, find the proper table (on pages 26–45) for your payroll period and the employee's marital status as shown on his or her Form W-4. Then, based on the number of withholding allowances claimed on the Form W-4 and the amount of wages, find the amount of federal income tax to withhold. If your employee is claiming more than 10 withholding allowances, see below.

If you can't use the wage bracket tables because wages exceed the amount shown in the last bracket of the table, use the percentage method of withholding described later in this section. Be sure to reduce wages by the amount of total withholding allowances (shown in the table below) before using the percentage method tables on pages 24 and 25.

Adjusting wage bracket withholding for employees claiming over 10 withholding allowances. To adapt the wage bracket tables for employees who are claiming over 10 allowances, follow these steps.

1. Multiply the number of withholding allowances that is over 10 by the allowance value for the payroll period. The allowance values are in the Percentage Method—2016 Amount for One Withholding Allowance table shown later.

2. Subtract the result from the employee's wages.

3. On this amount, find and withhold the tax in the column for 10 allowances.

This is a voluntary method. If you use the wage bracket tables, you may continue to withhold the amount in the "10" column when your employee has more than 10 allowances, using the method above. You can also use the other methods described later.

Percentage Method

If you don't want to use the wage bracket tables on pages 26–45 to figure how much federal income tax to withhold, you can use the percentage method based on the table on this page and the appropriate rate table. This method works for any number of withholding allowances the employee claims and any amount of wages.

Use these steps to figure the federal income tax to withhold under the percentage method.

1. Multiply one withholding allowance (see table later) by the number of allowances the employee claims.

2. Subtract that amount from the employee's wages.

3. Determine the amount to withhold from the appropriate table on pages 24 and 25.

Percentage Method—2016 Amount for One Withholding Allowance

Payroll Period	One Withholding Allowance
Weekly	$ 77.90
Biweekly	155.80
Semimonthly	168.80
Monthly	337.50
Quarterly	1,012.50
Semiannually	2,025.00
Annually	4,050.00
Daily or miscellaneous (each day of the payroll period)	15.60

Example. An unmarried employee is paid $800 weekly. This employee has a Form W-4 in effect claiming two withholding allowances. Using the percentage method, figure the federal income tax withholding as follows.

1.	Total wage payment		$800.00
2.	One allowance	$77.90	
3.	Allowances claimed on Form W-4 . .	2	
4.	Multiply line 2 by line 3		$155.80
5.	Amount subject to withholding (subtract line 4 from line 1)		$644.20
6.	Tax to be withheld on $644.20 from Table 1—single person, page 24 . . .		$81.23

To figure the federal income tax to withhold, you may reduce the last digit of the wages to zero, or figure the wages to the nearest dollar.

Annual income tax withholding. Figure the federal income tax to withhold on annual wages under the *Percentage Method* for an annual payroll period. Then prorate the tax back to the payroll period.

Example. A married person claims four withholding allowances. She is paid $1,000 a week. Multiply the weekly wages by 52 weeks to figure the annual wage of $52,000. Subtract $16,200 (the value of four withholding allowances annually) for a balance of $35,800. Using column (b) of Table 7—Annual Payroll Period on page 25, the annual federal income tax withholding is $3,160.00. Divide the annual amount by 52. The weekly federal income tax to withhold is $60.77.

Alternative Methods of Federal Income Tax Withholding

Rather than the *Percentage Method* or *Wage Bracket Method* described above, you can use an alternative method to withhold federal income tax. Section 9 of Pub. 15-A describes these alternative methods.

(For Wages Paid in 2016)

TABLE 1—WEEKLY Payroll Period

(a) SINGLE person (including head of household)—

If the amount of wages (after subtracting withholding allowances) is:		The amount of income tax to withhold is:	
Not over $43		$0	
Over—	**But not over—**		**of excess over—**
$43	—$222 . .	$0.00 plus 10%	—$43
$222	—$767 . .	$17.90 plus 15%	—$222
$767	—$1,796 . .	$99.65 plus 25%	—$767
$1,796	—$3,700 . .	$356.90 plus 28%	—$1,796
$3,700	—$7,992 . .	$890.02 plus 33%	—$3,700
$7,992	—$8,025 . .	$2,306.38 plus 35%	—$7,992
$8,025	. . . .	$2,317.93 plus 39.6%	—$8,025

(b) MARRIED person—

If the amount of wages (after subtracting withholding allowances) is:		The amount of income tax to withhold is:	
Not over $164		$0	
Over—	**But not over—**		**of excess over—**
$164	—$521 . .	$0.00 plus 10%	—$164
$521	—$1,613 . .	$35.70 plus 15%	—$521
$1,613	—$3,086 . .	$199.50 plus 25%	—$1,613
$3,086	—$4,615 . .	$567.75 plus 28%	—$3,086
$4,615	—$8,113 . .	$995.87 plus 33%	—$4,615
$8,113	—$9,144 . .	$2,150.21 plus 35%	—$8,113
$9,144	. . . .	$2,511.06 plus 39.6%	—$9,144

TABLE 2—BIWEEKLY Payroll Period

(a) SINGLE person (including head of household)—

If the amount of wages (after subtracting withholding allowances) is:		The amount of income tax to withhold is:	
Not over $87		$0	
Over—	**But not over—**		**of excess over—**
$87	—$443 . .	$0.00 plus 10%	—$87
$443	—$1,535 . .	$35.60 plus 15%	—$443
$1,535	—$3,592 . .	$199.40 plus 25%	—$1,535
$3,592	—$7,400 . .	$713.65 plus 28%	—$3,592
$7,400	—$15,985 . .	$1,779.89 plus 33%	—$7,400
$15,985	—$16,050 . .	$4,612.94 plus 35%	—$15,985
$16,050	. . . .	$4,635.69 plus 39.6%	—$16,050

(b) MARRIED person—

If the amount of wages (after subtracting withholding allowances) is:		The amount of income tax to withhold is:	
Not over $329		$0	
Over—	**But not over—**		**of excess over—**
$329	—$1,042 . .	$0.00 plus 10%	—$329
$1,042	—$3,225 . .	$71.30 plus 15%	—$1,042
$3,225	—$6,171 . .	$398.75 plus 25%	—$3,225
$6,171	—$9,231 . .	$1,135.25 plus 28%	—$6,171
$9,231	—$16,227 . .	$1,992.05 plus 33%	—$9,231
$16,227	—$18,288 . .	$4,300.73 plus 35%	—$16,227
$18,288	. . . .	$5,022.08 plus 39.6%	—$18,288

TABLE 3—SEMIMONTHLY Payroll Period

(a) SINGLE person (including head of household)—

If the amount of wages (after subtracting withholding allowances) is:		The amount of income tax to withhold is:	
Not over $94		$0	
Over—	**But not over—**		**of excess over—**
$94	—$480 . .	$0.00 plus 10%	—$94
$480	—$1,663 . .	$38.60 plus 15%	—$480
$1,663	—$3,892 . .	$216.05 plus 25%	—$1,663
$3,892	—$8,017 . .	$773.30 plus 28%	—$3,892
$8,017	—$17,317 . .	$1,928.30 plus 33%	—$8,017
$17,317	—$17,388 . .	$4,997.30 plus 35%	—$17,317
$17,388	. . . .	$5,022.15 plus 39.6%	—$17,388

(b) MARRIED person—

If the amount of wages (after subtracting withholding allowances) is:		The amount of income tax to withhold is:	
Not over $356		$0	
Over—	**But not over—**		**of excess over—**
$356	—$1,129 . .	$0.00 plus 10%	—$356
$1,129	—$3,494 . .	$77.30 plus 15%	—$1,129
$3,494	—$6,685 . .	$432.05 plus 25%	—$3,494
$6,685	—$10,000 . .	$1,229.80 plus 28%	—$6,685
$10,000	—$17,579 . .	$2,158.00 plus 33%	—$10,000
$17,579	—$19,813 . .	$4,659.07 plus 35%	—$17,579
$19,813	. . . .	$5,440.97 plus 39.6%	—$19,813

TABLE 4—MONTHLY Payroll Period

(a) SINGLE person (including head of household)—

If the amount of wages (after subtracting withholding allowances) is:		The amount of income tax to withhold is:	
Not over $188		$0	
Over—	**But not over—**		**of excess over—**
$188	—$960 . .	$0.00 plus 10%	—$188
$960	—$3,325 . .	$77.20 plus 15%	—$960
$3,325	—$7,783 . .	$431.95 plus 25%	—$3,325
$7,783	—$16,033 . .	$1,546.45 plus 28%	—$7,783
$16,033	—$34,633 . .	$3,856.45 plus 33%	—$16,033
$34,633	—$34,775 . .	$9,994.45 plus 35%	—$34,633
$34,775	. . . .	$10,044.15 plus 39.6%	—$34,775

(b) MARRIED person—

If the amount of wages (after subtracting withholding allowances) is:		The amount of income tax to withhold is:	
Not over $713		$0	
Over—	**But not over—**		**of excess over—**
$713	—$2,258 . .	$0.00 plus 10%	—$713
$2,258	—$6,988 . .	$154.50 plus 15%	—$2,258
$6,988	—$13,371 . .	$864.00 plus 25%	—$6,988
$13,371	—$20,000 . .	$2,459.75 plus 28%	—$13,371
$20,000	—$35,158 . .	$4,315.87 plus 33%	—$20,000
$35,158	—$39,625 . .	$9,318.01 plus 35%	—$35,158
$39,625	. . . .	$10,881.46 plus 39.6%	—$39,625

Percentage Method Tables for Income Tax Withholding (continued)

(For Wages Paid in 2016)

TABLE 5—QUARTERLY Payroll Period

(a) SINGLE person (including head of household)—

If the amount of wages (after subtracting withholding allowances) is: Not over $563 . . . . $0

The amount of income tax to withhold is:

Over—	But not over—		of excess over—
$563	—$2,881	$0.00 plus 10%	—$563
$2,881	—$9,975	$231.80 plus 15%	—$2,881
$9,975	—$23,350	$1,295.90 plus 25%	—$9,975
$23,350	—$48,100	$4,639.65 plus 28%	—$23,350
$48,100	—$103,900	$11,569.65 plus 33%	—$48,100
$103,900	—$104,325	$29,983.65 plus 35%	—$103,900
$104,325	. . . .	$30,132.40 plus 39.6%	—$104,325

(b) MARRIED person—

If the amount of wages (after subtracting withholding allowances) is: Not over $2,138 . . . . $0

The amount of income tax to withhold is:

Over—	But not over—		of excess over—
$2,138	—$6,775	$0.00 plus 10%	—$2,138
$6,775	—$20,963	$463.70 plus 15%	—$6,775
$20,963	—$40,113	$2,591.90 plus 25%	—$20,963
$40,113	—$60,000	$7,379.40 plus 28%	—$40,113
$60,000	—$105,475	$12,947.76 plus 33%	—$60,000
$105,475	—$118,875	$27,954.51 plus 35%	—$105,475
$118,875	. . . .	$32,644.51 plus 39.6%	—$118,875

TABLE 6—SEMIANNUAL Payroll Period

(a) SINGLE person (including head of household)—

If the amount of wages (after subtracting withholding allowances) is: Not over $1,125 . . . . $0

The amount of income tax to withhold is:

Over—	But not over—		of excess over—
$1,125	—$5,763	$0.00 plus 10%	—$1,125
$5,763	—$19,950	$463.80 plus 15%	—$5,763
$19,950	—$46,700	$2,591.85 plus 25%	—$19,950
$46,700	—$96,200	$9,279.35 plus 28%	—$46,700
$96,200	—$207,800	$23,139.35 plus 33%	—$96,200
$207,800	—$208,650	$59,967.35 plus 35%	—$207,800
$208,650	. . . .	$60,264.85 plus 39.6%	—$208,650

(b) MARRIED person—

If the amount of wages (after subtracting withholding allowances) is: Not over $4,275 . . . . $0

The amount of income tax to withhold is:

Over—	But not over—		of excess over—
$4,275	—$13,550	$0.00 plus 10%	—$4,275
$13,550	—$41,925	$927.50 plus 15%	—$13,550
$41,925	—$80,225	$5,183.75 plus 25%	—$41,925
$80,225	—$120,000	$14,758.75 plus 28%	—$80,225
$120,000	—$210,950	$25,895.75 plus 33%	—$120,000
$210,950	—$237,750	$55,909.25 plus 35%	—$210,950
$237,750	. . . .	$65,289.25 plus 39.6%	—$237,750

TABLE 7—ANNUAL Payroll Period

(a) SINGLE person (including head of household)—

If the amount of wages (after subtracting withholding allowances) is: Not over $2,250 . . . . $0

The amount of income tax to withhold is:

Over—	But not over—		of excess over—
$2,250	—$11,525	$0.00 plus 10%	—$2,250
$11,525	—$39,900	$927.50 plus 15%	—$11,525
$39,900	—$93,400	$5,183.75 plus 25%	—$39,900
$93,400	—$192,400	$18,558.75 plus 28%	—$93,400
$192,400	—$415,600	$46,278.75 plus 33%	—$192,400
$415,600	—$417,300	$119,934.75 plus 35%	—$415,600
$417,300	. . . .	$120,529.75 plus 39.6%	—$417,300

(b) MARRIED person—

If the amount of wages (after subtracting withholding allowances) is: Not over $8,550 . . . . $0

The amount of income tax to withhold is:

Over—	But not over—		of excess over—
$8,550	—$27,100	$0.00 plus 10%	—$8,550
$27,100	—$83,850	$1,855.00 plus 15%	—$27,100
$83,850	—$160,450	$10,367.50 plus 25%	—$83,850
$160,450	—$240,000	$29,517.50 plus 28%	—$160,450
$240,000	—$421,900	$51,791.50 plus 33%	—$240,000
$421,900	—$475,500	$111,818.50 plus 35%	—$421,900
$475,500	. . . .	$130,578.50 plus 39.6%	—$475,500

TABLE 8—DAILY or MISCELLANEOUS Payroll Period

(a) SINGLE person (including head of household)—

If the amount of wages (after subtracting withholding allowances) divided by the number of days in the payroll period is: Not over $8.70 . . . . $0

The amount of income tax to withhold per day is:

Over—	But not over—		of excess over—
$8.70	—$44.30	$0.00 plus 10%	—$8.70
$44.30	—$153.50	$3.56 plus 15%	—$44.30
$153.50	—$359.20	$19.94 plus 25%	—$153.50
$359.20	—$740.00	$71.37 plus 28%	—$359.20
$740.00	—$1,598.50	$177.99 plus 33%	—$740.00
$1,598.50	—$1,605.00	$461.30 plus 35%	—$1,598.50
$1,605.00	. . . .	$463.58 plus 39.6%	—$1,605.00

(b) MARRIED person—

If the amount of wages (after subtracting withholding allowances) divided by the number of days in the payroll period is: Not over $32.90 . . . . $0

The amount of income tax to withhold per day is:

Over—	But not over—		of excess over—
$32.90	—$104.20	$0.00 plus 10%	—$32.90
$104.20	—$322.50	$7.13 plus 15%	—$104.20
$322.50	—$617.10	$39.88 plus 25%	—$322.50
$617.10	—$923.10	$113.53 plus 28%	—$617.10
$923.10	—$1,622.70	$199.21 plus 33%	—$923.10
$1,622.70	—$1,828.80	$430.08 plus 35%	—$1,622.70
$1,828.80	. . . .	$502.22 plus 39.6%	—$1,828.80

Wage Bracket Method Tables for Income Tax Withholding

SINGLE Persons—WEEKLY Payroll Period

(For Wages Paid through December 31, 2016)

And the wages are—		And the number of withholding allowances claimed is—										
At least	But less than	0	1	2	3	4	5	6	7	8	9	10
		The amount of income tax to be withheld is—										
$0	$55	$0	$0	$0	$0	$0	$0	$0	$0	$0	$0	$0
55	60	1	0	0	0	0	0	0	0	0	0	0
60	65	2	0	0	0	0	0	0	0	0	0	0
65	70	2	0	0	0	0	0	0	0	0	0	0
70	75	3	0	0	0	0	0	0	0	0	0	0
75	80	3	0	0	0	0	0	0	0	0	0	0
80	85	4	0	0	0	0	0	0	0	0	0	0
85	90	4	0	0	0	0	0	0	0	0	0	0
90	95	5	0	0	0	0	0	0	0	0	0	0
95	100	5	0	0	0	0	0	0	0	0	0	0
100	105	6	0	0	0	0	0	0	0	0	0	0
105	110	6	0	0	0	0	0	0	0	0	0	0
110	115	7	0	0	0	0	0	0	0	0	0	0
115	120	7	0	0	0	0	0	0	0	0	0	0
120	125	8	0	0	0	0	0	0	0	0	0	0
125	130	8	1	0	0	0	0	0	0	0	0	0
130	135	9	1	0	0	0	0	0	0	0	0	0
135	140	9	2	0	0	0	0	0	0	0	0	0
140	145	10	2	0	0	0	0	0	0	0	0	0
145	150	10	3	0	0	0	0	0	0	0	0	0
150	155	11	3	0	0	0	0	0	0	0	0	0
155	160	11	4	0	0	0	0	0	0	0	0	0
160	165	12	4	0	0	0	0	0	0	0	0	0
165	170	12	5	0	0	0	0	0	0	0	0	0
170	175	13	5	0	0	0	0	0	0	0	0	0
175	180	13	6	0	0	0	0	0	0	0	0	0
180	185	14	6	0	0	0	0	0	0	0	0	0
185	190	14	7	0	0	0	0	0	0	0	0	0
190	195	15	7	0	0	0	0	0	0	0	0	0
195	200	15	8	0	0	0	0	0	0	0	0	0
200	210	16	8	1	0	0	0	0	0	0	0	0
210	220	17	9	2	0	0	0	0	0	0	0	0
220	230	18	10	3	0	0	0	0	0	0	0	0
230	240	20	11	4	0	0	0	0	0	0	0	0
240	250	21	12	5	0	0	0	0	0	0	0	0
250	260	23	13	6	0	0	0	0	0	0	0	0
260	270	24	14	7	0	0	0	0	0	0	0	0
270	280	26	15	8	0	0	0	0	0	0	0	0
280	290	27	16	9	1	0	0	0	0	0	0	0
290	300	29	17	10	2	0	0	0	0	0	0	0
300	310	30	19	11	3	0	0	0	0	0	0	0
310	320	32	20	12	4	0	0	0	0	0	0	0
320	330	33	22	13	5	0	0	0	0	0	0	0
330	340	35	23	14	6	0	0	0	0	0	0	0
340	350	36	25	15	7	0	0	0	0	0	0	0
350	360	38	26	16	8	0	0	0	0	0	0	0
360	370	39	28	17	9	1	0	0	0	0	0	0
370	380	41	29	18	10	2	0	0	0	0	0	0
380	390	42	31	19	11	3	0	0	0	0	0	0
390	400	44	32	20	12	4	0	0	0	0	0	0
400	410	45	34	22	13	5	0	0	0	0	0	0
410	420	47	35	23	14	6	0	0	0	0	0	0
420	430	48	37	25	15	7	0	0	0	0	0	0
430	440	50	38	26	16	8	0	0	0	0	0	0
440	450	51	40	28	17	9	1	0	0	0	0	0
450	460	53	41	29	18	10	2	0	0	0	0	0
460	470	54	43	31	19	11	3	0	0	0	0	0
470	480	56	44	32	21	12	4	0	0	0	0	0
480	490	57	46	34	22	13	5	0	0	0	0	0
490	500	59	47	35	24	14	6	0	0	0	0	0
500	510	60	49	37	25	15	7	0	0	0	0	0
510	520	62	50	38	27	16	8	0	0	0	0	0
520	530	63	52	40	28	17	9	1	0	0	0	0
530	540	65	53	41	30	18	10	2	0	0	0	0
540	550	66	55	43	31	20	11	3	0	0	0	0
550	560	68	56	44	33	21	12	4	0	0	0	0
560	570	69	58	46	34	23	13	5	0	0	0	0
570	580	71	59	47	36	24	14	6	0	0	0	0
580	590	72	61	49	37	26	15	7	0	0	0	0
590	600	74	62	50	39	27	16	8	1	0	0	0

Wage Bracket Method Tables for Income Tax Withholding

SINGLE Persons—WEEKLY Payroll Period

(For Wages Paid through December 31, 2016)

And the wages are—		And the number of withholding allowances claimed is—										
At least	But less than	0	1	2	3	4	5	6	7	8	9	10
		The amount of income tax to be withheld is—										
$600	$610	$75	$64	$52	$40	$29	$17	$9	$2	$0	$0	$0
610	620	77	65	53	42	30	18	10	3	0	0	0
620	630	78	67	55	43	32	20	11	4	0	0	0
630	640	80	68	56	45	33	21	12	5	0	0	0
640	650	81	70	58	46	35	23	13	6	0	0	0
650	660	83	71	59	48	36	24	14	7	0	0	0
660	670	84	73	61	49	38	26	15	8	0	0	0
670	680	86	74	62	51	39	27	16	9	1	0	0
680	690	87	76	64	52	41	29	17	10	2	0	0
690	700	89	77	65	54	42	30	19	11	3	0	0
700	710	90	79	67	55	44	32	20	12	4	0	0
710	720	92	80	68	57	45	33	22	13	5	0	0
720	730	93	82	70	58	47	35	23	14	6	0	0
730	740	95	83	71	60	48	36	25	15	7	0	0
740	750	96	85	73	61	50	38	26	16	8	0	0
750	760	98	86	74	63	51	39	28	17	9	1	0
760	770	99	88	76	64	53	41	29	18	10	2	0
770	780	102	89	77	66	54	42	31	19	11	3	0
780	790	104	91	79	67	56	44	32	21	12	4	0
790	800	107	92	80	69	57	45	34	22	13	5	0
800	810	109	94	82	70	59	47	35	24	14	6	0
810	820	112	95	83	72	60	48	37	25	15	7	0
820	830	114	97	85	73	62	50	38	27	16	8	0
830	840	117	98	86	75	63	51	40	28	17	9	1
840	850	119	100	88	76	65	53	41	30	18	10	2
850	860	122	102	89	78	66	54	43	31	19	11	3
860	870	124	105	91	79	68	56	44	33	21	12	4
870	880	127	107	92	81	69	57	46	34	22	13	5
880	890	129	110	94	82	71	59	47	36	24	14	6
890	900	132	112	95	84	72	60	49	37	25	15	7
900	910	134	115	97	85	74	62	50	39	27	16	8
910	920	137	117	98	87	75	63	52	40	28	17	9
920	930	139	120	100	88	77	65	53	42	30	18	10
930	940	142	122	103	90	78	66	55	43	31	20	11
940	950	144	125	105	91	80	68	56	45	33	21	12
950	960	147	127	108	93	81	69	58	46	34	23	13
960	970	149	130	110	94	83	71	59	48	36	24	14
970	980	152	132	113	96	84	72	61	49	37	26	15
980	990	154	135	115	97	86	74	62	51	39	27	16
990	1,000	157	137	118	99	87	75	64	52	40	29	17
1,000	1,010	159	140	120	101	89	77	65	54	42	30	19
1,010	1,020	162	142	123	103	90	78	67	55	43	32	20
1,020	1,030	164	145	125	106	92	80	68	57	45	33	22
1,030	1,040	167	147	128	108	93	81	70	58	46	35	23
1,040	1,050	169	150	130	111	95	83	71	60	48	36	25
1,050	1,060	172	152	133	113	96	84	73	61	49	38	26
1,060	1,070	174	155	135	116	98	86	74	63	51	39	28
1,070	1,080	177	157	138	118	99	87	76	64	52	41	29
1,080	1,090	179	160	140	121	101	89	77	66	54	42	31
1,090	1,100	182	162	143	123	104	90	79	67	55	44	32
1,100	1,110	184	165	145	126	106	92	80	69	57	45	34
1,110	1,120	187	167	148	128	109	93	82	70	58	47	35
1,120	1,130	189	170	150	131	111	95	83	72	60	48	37
1,130	1,140	192	172	153	133	114	96	85	73	61	50	38
1,140	1,150	194	175	155	136	116	98	86	75	63	51	40
1,150	1,160	197	177	158	138	119	99	88	76	64	53	41
1,160	1,170	199	180	160	141	121	102	89	78	66	54	43
1,170	1,180	202	182	163	143	124	104	91	79	67	56	44
1,180	1,190	204	185	165	146	126	107	92	81	69	57	46
1,190	1,200	207	187	168	148	129	109	94	82	70	59	47
1,200	1,210	209	190	170	151	131	112	95	84	72	60	49
1,210	1,220	212	192	173	153	134	114	97	85	73	62	50
1,220	1,230	214	195	175	156	136	117	98	87	75	63	52
1,230	1,240	217	197	178	158	139	119	100	88	76	65	53
1,240	1,250	219	200	180	161	141	122	102	90	78	66	55

$1,250 and over	Use Table 1(a) for a **SINGLE person** on page 24. Also see the instructions on page 23.

Wage Bracket Method Tables for Income Tax Withholding

MARRIED Persons—WEEKLY Payroll Period

(For Wages Paid through December 31, 2016)

And the wages are–		And the number of withholding allowances claimed is—										
At least	But less than	0	1	2	3	4	5	6	7	8	9	10
		The amount of income tax to be withheld is—										
$ 0	$170	$0	$0	$0	$0	$0	$0	$0	$0	$0	$0	$0
170	175	1	0	0	0	0	0	0	0	0	0	0
175	180	1	0	0	0	0	0	0	0	0	0	0
180	185	2	0	0	0	0	0	0	0	0	0	0
185	190	2	0	0	0	0	0	0	0	0	0	0
190	195	3	0	0	0	0	0	0	0	0	0	0
195	200	3	0	0	0	0	0	0	0	0	0	0
200	210	4	0	0	0	0	0	0	0	0	0	0
210	220	5	0	0	0	0	0	0	0	0	0	0
220	230	6	0	0	0	0	0	0	0	0	0	0
230	240	7	0	0	0	0	0	0	0	0	0	0
240	250	8	0	0	0	0	0	0	0	0	0	0
250	260	9	1	0	0	0	0	0	0	0	0	0
260	270	10	2	0	0	0	0	0	0	0	0	0
270	280	11	3	0	0	0	0	0	0	0	0	0
280	290	12	4	0	0	0	0	0	0	0	0	0
290	300	13	5	0	0	0	0	0	0	0	0	0
300	310	14	6	0	0	0	0	0	0	0	0	0
310	320	15	7	0	0	0	0	0	0	0	0	0
320	330	16	8	0	0	0	0	0	0	0	0	0
330	340	17	9	1	0	0	0	0	0	0	0	0
340	350	18	10	2	0	0	0	0	0	0	0	0
350	360	19	11	3	0	0	0	0	0	0	0	0
360	370	20	12	4	0	0	0	0	0	0	0	0
370	380	21	13	5	0	0	0	0	0	0	0	0
380	390	22	14	6	0	0	0	0	0	0	0	0
390	400	23	15	7	0	0	0	0	0	0	0	0
400	410	24	16	8	1	0	0	0	0	0	0	0
410	420	25	17	9	2	0	0	0	0	0	0	0
420	430	26	18	10	3	0	0	0	0	0	0	0
430	440	27	19	11	4	0	0	0	0	0	0	0
440	450	28	20	12	5	0	0	0	0	0	0	0
450	460	29	21	13	6	0	0	0	0	0	0	0
460	470	30	22	14	7	0	0	0	0	0	0	0
470	480	31	23	15	8	0	0	0	0	0	0	0
480	490	32	24	16	9	1	0	0	0	0	0	0
490	500	33	25	17	10	2	0	0	0	0	0	0
500	510	34	26	18	11	3	0	0	0	0	0	0
510	520	35	27	19	12	4	0	0	0	0	0	0
520	530	36	28	20	13	5	0	0	0	0	0	0
530	540	38	29	21	14	6	0	0	0	0	0	0
540	550	39	30	22	15	7	0	0	0	0	0	0
550	560	41	31	23	16	8	0	0	0	0	0	0
560	570	42	32	24	17	9	1	0	0	0	0	0
570	580	44	33	25	18	10	2	0	0	0	0	0
580	590	45	34	26	19	11	3	0	0	0	0	0
590	600	47	35	27	20	12	4	0	0	0	0	0
600	610	48	37	28	21	13	5	0	0	0	0	0
610	620	50	38	29	22	14	6	0	0	0	0	0
620	630	51	40	30	23	15	7	0	0	0	0	0
630	640	53	41	31	24	16	8	0	0	0	0	0
640	650	54	43	32	25	17	9	1	0	0	0	0
650	660	56	44	33	26	18	10	2	0	0	0	0
660	670	57	46	34	27	19	11	3	0	0	0	0
670	680	59	47	35	28	20	12	4	0	0	0	0
680	690	60	49	37	29	21	13	5	0	0	0	0
690	700	62	50	38	30	22	14	6	0	0	0	0
700	710	63	52	40	31	23	15	7	0	0	0	0
710	720	65	53	41	32	24	16	8	1	0	0	0
720	730	66	55	43	33	25	17	9	2	0	0	0
730	740	68	56	44	34	26	18	10	3	0	0	0
740	750	69	58	46	35	27	19	11	4	0	0	0
750	760	71	59	47	36	28	20	12	5	0	0	0
760	770	72	61	49	37	29	21	13	6	0	0	0
770	780	74	62	50	39	30	22	14	7	0	0	0
780	790	75	64	52	40	31	23	15	8	0	0	0
790	800	77	65	53	42	32	24	16	9	1	0	0

Wage Bracket Method Tables for Income Tax Withholding

MARRIED Persons—WEEKLY Payroll Period

(For Wages Paid through December 31, 2016)

And the wages are—		And the number of withholding allowances claimed is—										
At least	But less than	0	1	2	3	4	5	6	7	8	9	10
		The amount of income tax to be withheld is—										
$800	$810	$78	$67	$55	$43	$33	$25	$17	$10	$2	$0	$0
810	820	80	68	56	45	34	26	18	11	3	0	0
820	830	81	70	58	46	35	27	19	12	4	0	0
830	840	83	71	59	48	36	28	20	13	5	0	0
840	850	84	73	61	49	38	29	21	14	6	0	0
850	860	86	74	62	51	39	30	22	15	7	0	0
860	870	87	76	64	52	41	31	23	16	8	0	0
870	880	89	77	65	54	42	32	24	17	9	1	0
880	890	90	79	67	55	44	33	25	18	10	2	0
890	900	92	80	68	57	45	34	26	19	11	3	0
900	910	93	82	70	58	47	35	27	20	12	4	0
910	920	95	83	71	60	48	36	28	21	13	5	0
920	930	96	85	73	61	50	38	29	22	14	6	0
930	940	98	86	74	63	51	39	30	23	15	7	0
940	950	99	88	76	64	53	41	31	24	16	8	0
950	960	101	89	77	66	54	42	32	25	17	9	1
960	970	102	91	79	67	56	44	33	26	18	10	2
970	980	104	92	80	69	57	45	34	27	19	11	3
980	990	105	94	82	70	59	47	35	28	20	12	4
990	1,000	107	95	83	72	60	48	37	29	21	13	5
1,000	1,010	108	97	85	73	62	50	38	30	22	14	6
1,010	1,020	110	98	86	75	63	51	40	31	23	15	7
1,020	1,030	111	100	88	76	65	53	41	32	24	16	8
1,030	1,040	113	101	89	78	66	54	43	33	25	17	9
1,040	1,050	114	103	91	79	68	56	44	34	26	18	10
1,050	1,060	116	104	92	81	69	57	46	35	27	19	11
1,060	1,070	117	106	94	82	71	59	47	36	28	20	12
1,070	1,080	119	107	95	84	72	60	49	37	29	21	13
1,080	1,090	120	109	97	85	74	62	50	38	30	22	14
1,090	1,100	122	110	98	87	75	63	52	40	31	23	15
1,100	1,110	123	112	100	88	77	65	53	41	32	24	16
1,110	1,120	125	113	101	90	78	66	55	43	33	25	17
1,120	1,130	126	115	103	91	80	68	56	44	34	26	18
1,130	1,140	128	116	104	93	81	69	58	46	35	27	19
1,140	1,150	129	118	106	94	83	71	59	47	36	28	20
1,150	1,160	131	119	107	96	84	72	61	49	37	29	21
1,160	1,170	132	121	109	97	86	74	62	50	39	30	22
1,170	1,180	134	122	110	99	87	75	64	52	40	31	23
1,180	1,190	135	124	112	100	89	77	65	53	42	32	24
1,190	1,200	137	125	113	102	90	78	67	55	43	33	25
1,200	1,210	138	127	115	103	92	80	68	56	45	34	26
1,210	1,220	140	128	116	105	93	81	70	58	46	35	27
1,220	1,230	141	130	118	106	95	83	71	59	48	36	28
1,230	1,240	143	131	119	108	96	84	73	61	49	38	29
1,240	1,250	144	133	121	109	98	86	74	62	51	39	30
1,250	1,260	146	134	122	111	99	87	76	64	52	41	31
1,260	1,270	147	136	124	112	101	89	77	65	54	42	32
1,270	1,280	149	137	125	114	102	90	79	67	55	44	33
1,280	1,290	150	139	127	115	104	92	80	68	57	45	34
1,290	1,300	152	140	128	117	105	93	82	70	58	47	35
1,300	1,310	153	142	130	118	107	95	83	71	60	48	36
1,310	1,320	155	143	131	120	108	96	85	73	61	50	38
1,320	1,330	156	145	133	121	110	98	86	74	63	51	39
1,330	1,340	158	146	134	123	111	99	88	76	64	53	41
1,340	1,350	159	148	136	124	113	101	89	77	66	54	42
1,350	1,360	161	149	137	126	114	102	91	79	67	56	44
1,360	1,370	162	151	139	127	116	104	92	80	69	57	45
1,370	1,380	164	152	140	129	117	105	94	82	70	59	47
1,380	1,390	165	154	142	130	119	107	95	83	72	60	48
1,390	1,400	167	155	143	132	120	108	97	85	73	62	50
1,400	1,410	168	157	145	133	122	110	98	86	75	63	51
1,410	1,420	170	158	146	135	123	111	100	88	76	65	53
1,420	1,430	171	160	148	136	125	113	101	89	78	66	54
1,430	1,440	173	161	149	138	126	114	103	91	79	68	56
1,440	1,450	174	163	151	139	128	116	104	92	81	69	57
1,450	1,460	176	164	152	141	129	117	106	94	82	71	59
1,460	1,470	177	166	154	142	131	119	107	95	84	72	60
1,470	1,480	179	167	155	144	132	120	109	97	85	74	62
1,480	1,490	180	169	157	145	134	122	110	98	87	75	63

$1,490 and over   Use Table 1(b) for a **MARRIED person** on page 24. Also see the instructions on page 23.

Wage Bracket Method Tables for Income Tax Withholding

SINGLE Persons—**BIWEEKLY** Payroll Period

(For Wages Paid through December 31, 2016)

And the wages are—		And the number of withholding allowances claimed is—										
At least	But less than	0	1	2	3	4	5	6	7	8	9	10
		The amount of income tax to be withheld is—										
$ 0	$105	$0	$0	$0	$0	$0	$0	$0	$0	$0	$0	$0
105	110	2	0	0	0	0	0	0	0	0	0	0
110	115	3	0	0	0	0	0	0	0	0	0	0
115	120	3	0	0	0	0	0	0	0	0	0	0
120	125	4	0	0	0	0	0	0	0	0	0	0
125	130	4	0	0	0	0	0	0	0	0	0	0
130	135	5	0	0	0	0	0	0	0	0	0	0
135	140	5	0	0	0	0	0	0	0	0	0	0
140	145	6	0	0	0	0	0	0	0	0	0	0
145	150	6	0	0	0	0	0	0	0	0	0	0
150	155	7	0	0	0	0	0	0	0	0	0	0
155	160	7	0	0	0	0	0	0	0	0	0	0
160	165	8	0	0	0	0	0	0	0	0	0	0
165	170	8	0	0	0	0	0	0	0	0	0	0
170	175	9	0	0	0	0	0	0	0	0	0	0
175	180	9	0	0	0	0	0	0	0	0	0	0
180	185	10	0	0	0	0	0	0	0	0	0	0
185	190	10	0	0	0	0	0	0	0	0	0	0
190	195	11	0	0	0	0	0	0	0	0	0	0
195	200	11	0	0	0	0	0	0	0	0	0	0
200	205	12	0	0	0	0	0	0	0	0	0	0
205	210	12	0	0	0	0	0	0	0	0	0	0
210	215	13	0	0	0	0	0	0	0	0	0	0
215	220	13	0	0	0	0	0	0	0	0	0	0
220	225	14	0	0	0	0	0	0	0	0	0	0
225	230	14	0	0	0	0	0	0	0	0	0	0
230	235	15	0	0	0	0	0	0	0	0	0	0
235	240	15	0	0	0	0	0	0	0	0	0	0
240	245	16	0	0	0	0	0	0	0	0	0	0
245	250	16	1	0	0	0	0	0	0	0	0	0
250	260	17	1	0	0	0	0	0	0	0	0	0
260	270	18	2	0	0	0	0	0	0	0	0	0
270	280	19	3	0	0	0	0	0	0	0	0	0
280	290	20	4	0	0	0	0	0	0	0	0	0
290	300	21	5	0	0	0	0	0	0	0	0	0
300	310	22	6	0	0	0	0	0	0	0	0	0
310	320	23	7	0	0	0	0	0	0	0	0	0
320	330	24	8	0	0	0	0	0	0	0	0	0
330	340	25	9	0	0	0	0	0	0	0	0	0
340	350	26	10	0	0	0	0	0	0	0	0	0
350	360	27	11	0	0	0	0	0	0	0	0	0
360	370	28	12	0	0	0	0	0	0	0	0	0
370	380	29	13	0	0	0	0	0	0	0	0	0
380	390	30	14	0	0	0	0	0	0	0	0	0
390	400	31	15	0	0	0	0	0	0	0	0	0
400	410	32	16	1	0	0	0	0	0	0	0	0
410	420	33	17	2	0	0	0	0	0	0	0	0
420	430	34	18	3	0	0	0	0	0	0	0	0
430	440	35	19	4	0	0	0	0	0	0	0	0
440	450	36	20	5	0	0	0	0	0	0	0	0
450	460	37	21	6	0	0	0	0	0	0	0	0
460	470	39	22	7	0	0	0	0	0	0	0	0
470	480	40	23	8	0	0	0	0	0	0	0	0
480	490	42	24	9	0	0	0	0	0	0	0	0
490	500	43	25	10	0	0	0	0	0	0	0	0
500	520	46	27	11	0	0	0	0	0	0	0	0
520	540	49	29	13	0	0	0	0	0	0	0	0
540	560	52	31	15	0	0	0	0	0	0	0	0
560	580	55	33	17	2	0	0	0	0	0	0	0
580	600	58	35	19	4	0	0	0	0	0	0	0
600	620	61	37	21	6	0	0	0	0	0	0	0
620	640	64	40	23	8	0	0	0	0	0	0	0
640	660	67	43	25	10	0	0	0	0	0	0	0
660	680	70	46	27	12	0	0	0	0	0	0	0
680	700	73	49	29	14	0	0	0	0	0	0	0
700	720	76	52	31	16	0	0	0	0	0	0	0
720	740	79	55	33	18	2	0	0	0	0	0	0
740	760	82	58	35	20	4	0	0	0	0	0	0
760	780	85	61	38	22	6	0	0	0	0	0	0
780	800	88	64	41	24	8	0	0	0	0	0	0

Publication 51 (2016)

Wage Bracket Method Tables for Income Tax Withholding

SINGLE Persons—BIWEEKLY Payroll Period

(For Wages Paid through December 31, 2016)

And the wages are–		And the number of withholding allowances claimed is—										
At least	But less than	0	1	2	3	4	5	6	7	8	9	10
		The amount of income tax to be withheld is—										
$800	$820	$91	$67	$44	$26	$10	$0	$0	$0	$0	$0	$0
820	840	94	70	47	28	12	0	0	0	0	0	0
840	860	97	73	50	30	14	0	0	0	0	0	0
860	880	100	76	53	32	16	0	0	0	0	0	0
880	900	103	79	56	34	18	2	0	0	0	0	0
900	920	106	82	59	36	20	4	0	0	0	0	0
920	940	109	85	62	39	22	6	0	0	0	0	0
940	960	112	88	65	42	24	8	0	0	0	0	0
960	980	115	91	68	45	26	10	0	0	0	0	0
980	1,000	118	94	71	48	28	12	0	0	0	0	0
1,000	1,020	121	97	74	51	30	14	0	0	0	0	0
1,020	1,040	124	100	77	54	32	16	1	0	0	0	0
1,040	1,060	127	103	80	57	34	18	3	0	0	0	0
1,060	1,080	130	106	83	60	36	20	5	0	0	0	0
1,080	1,100	133	109	86	63	39	22	7	0	0	0	0
1,100	1,120	136	112	89	66	42	24	9	0	0	0	0
1,120	1,140	139	115	92	69	45	26	11	0	0	0	0
1,140	1,160	142	118	95	72	48	28	13	0	0	0	0
1,160	1,180	145	121	98	75	51	30	15	0	0	0	0
1,180	1,200	148	124	101	78	54	32	17	1	0	0	0
1,200	1,220	151	127	104	81	57	34	19	3	0	0	0
1,220	1,240	154	130	107	84	60	37	21	5	0	0	0
1,240	1,260	157	133	110	87	63	40	23	7	0	0	0
1,260	1,280	160	136	113	90	66	43	25	9	0	0	0
1,280	1,300	163	139	116	93	69	46	27	11	0	0	0
1,300	1,320	166	142	119	96	72	49	29	13	0	0	0
1,320	1,340	169	145	122	99	75	52	31	15	0	0	0
1,340	1,360	172	148	125	102	78	55	33	17	2	0	0
1,360	1,380	175	151	128	105	81	58	35	19	4	0	0
1,380	1,400	178	154	131	108	84	61	37	21	6	0	0
1,400	1,420	181	157	134	111	87	64	40	23	8	0	0
1,420	1,440	184	160	137	114	90	67	43	25	10	0	0
1,440	1,460	187	163	140	117	93	70	46	27	12	0	0
1,460	1,480	190	166	143	120	96	73	49	29	14	0	0
1,480	1,500	193	169	146	123	99	76	52	31	16	0	0
1,500	1,520	196	172	149	126	102	79	55	33	18	2	0
1,520	1,540	199	175	152	129	105	82	58	35	20	4	0
1,540	1,560	203	178	155	132	108	85	61	38	22	6	0
1,560	1,580	208	181	158	135	111	88	64	41	24	8	0
1,580	1,600	213	184	161	138	114	91	67	44	26	10	0
1,600	1,620	218	187	164	141	117	94	70	47	28	12	0
1,620	1,640	223	190	167	144	120	97	73	50	30	14	0
1,640	1,660	228	193	170	147	123	100	76	53	32	16	1
1,660	1,680	233	196	173	150	126	103	79	56	34	18	3
1,680	1,700	238	199	176	153	129	106	82	59	36	20	5
1,700	1,720	243	204	179	156	132	109	85	62	39	22	7
1,720	1,740	248	209	182	159	135	112	88	65	42	24	9
1,740	1,760	253	214	185	162	138	115	91	68	45	26	11
1,760	1,780	258	219	188	165	141	118	94	71	48	28	13
1,780	1,800	263	224	191	168	144	121	97	74	51	30	15
1,800	1,820	268	229	194	171	147	124	100	77	54	32	17
1,820	1,840	273	234	197	174	150	127	103	80	57	34	19
1,840	1,860	278	239	200	177	153	130	106	83	60	36	21
1,860	1,880	283	244	205	180	156	133	109	86	63	39	23
1,880	1,900	288	249	210	183	159	136	112	89	66	42	25
1,900	1,920	293	254	215	186	162	139	115	92	69	45	27
1,920	1,940	298	259	220	189	165	142	118	95	72	48	29
1,940	1,960	303	264	225	192	168	145	121	98	75	51	31
1,960	1,980	308	269	230	195	171	148	124	101	78	54	33
1,980	2,000	313	274	235	198	174	151	127	104	81	57	35
2,000	2,020	318	279	240	201	177	154	130	107	84	60	37
2,020	2,040	323	284	245	206	180	157	133	110	87	63	40
2,040	2,060	328	289	250	211	183	160	136	113	90	66	43
2,060	2,080	333	294	255	216	186	163	139	116	93	69	46
2,080	2,100	338	299	260	221	189	166	142	119	96	72	49

$2,100 and over   Use Table 2(a) for a **SINGLE person** on page 24. Also see the instructions on page 23.

Wage Bracket Method Tables for Income Tax Withholding

MARRIED Persons—BIWEEKLY Payroll Period

(For Wages Paid through December 31, 2016)

And the wages are–		And the number of withholding allowances claimed is—										
At least	But less than	0	1	2	3	4	5	6	7	8	9	10
		The amount of income tax to be withheld is—										
$ 0	$340	$0	$0	$0	$0	$0	$0	$0	$0	$0	$0	$0
340	350	2	0	0	0	0	0	0	0	0	0	0
350	360	3	0	0	0	0	0	0	0	0	0	0
360	370	4	0	0	0	0	0	0	0	0	0	0
370	380	5	0	0	0	0	0	0	0	0	0	0
380	390	6	0	0	0	0	0	0	0	0	0	0
390	400	7	0	0	0	0	0	0	0	0	0	0
400	410	8	0	0	0	0	0	0	0	0	0	0
410	420	9	0	0	0	0	0	0	0	0	0	0
420	430	10	0	0	0	0	0	0	0	0	0	0
430	440	11	0	0	0	0	0	0	0	0	0	0
440	450	12	0	0	0	0	0	0	0	0	0	0
450	460	13	0	0	0	0	0	0	0	0	0	0
460	470	14	0	0	0	0	0	0	0	0	0	0
470	480	15	0	0	0	0	0	0	0	0	0	0
480	490	16	0	0	0	0	0	0	0	0	0	0
490	500	17	1	0	0	0	0	0	0	0	0	0
500	520	18	3	0	0	0	0	0	0	0	0	0
520	540	20	5	0	0	0	0	0	0	0	0	0
540	560	22	7	0	0	0	0	0	0	0	0	0
560	580	24	9	0	0	0	0	0	0	0	0	0
580	600	26	11	0	0	0	0	0	0	0	0	0
600	620	28	13	0	0	0	0	0	0	0	0	0
620	640	30	15	0	0	0	0	0	0	0	0	0
640	660	32	17	1	0	0	0	0	0	0	0	0
660	680	34	19	3	0	0	0	0	0	0	0	0
680	700	36	21	5	0	0	0	0	0	0	0	0
700	720	38	23	7	0	0	0	0	0	0	0	0
720	740	40	25	9	0	0	0	0	0	0	0	0
740	760	42	27	11	0	0	0	0	0	0	0	0
760	780	44	29	13	0	0	0	0	0	0	0	0
780	800	46	31	15	0	0	0	0	0	0	0	0
800	820	48	33	17	1	0	0	0	0	0	0	0
820	840	50	35	19	3	0	0	0	0	0	0	0
840	860	52	37	21	5	0	0	0	0	0	0	0
860	880	54	39	23	7	0	0	0	0	0	0	0
880	900	56	41	25	9	0	0	0	0	0	0	0
900	920	58	43	27	11	0	0	0	0	0	0	0
920	940	60	45	29	13	0	0	0	0	0	0	0
940	960	62	47	31	15	0	0	0	0	0	0	0
960	980	64	49	33	17	2	0	0	0	0	0	0
980	1,000	66	51	35	19	4	0	0	0	0	0	0
1,000	1,020	68	53	37	21	6	0	0	0	0	0	0
1,020	1,040	70	55	39	23	8	0	0	0	0	0	0
1,040	1,060	73	57	41	25	10	0	0	0	0	0	0
1,060	1,080	76	59	43	27	12	0	0	0	0	0	0
1,080	1,100	79	61	45	29	14	0	0	0	0	0	0
1,100	1,120	82	63	47	31	16	0	0	0	0	0	0
1,120	1,140	85	65	49	33	18	2	0	0	0	0	0
1,140	1,160	88	67	51	35	20	4	0	0	0	0	0
1,160	1,180	91	69	53	37	22	6	0	0	0	0	0
1,180	1,200	94	71	55	39	24	8	0	0	0	0	0
1,200	1,220	97	73	57	41	26	10	0	0	0	0	0
1,220	1,240	100	76	59	43	28	12	0	0	0	0	0
1,240	1,260	103	79	61	45	30	14	0	0	0	0	0
1,260	1,280	106	82	63	47	32	16	1	0	0	0	0
1,280	1,300	109	85	65	49	34	18	3	0	0	0	0
1,300	1,320	112	88	67	51	36	20	5	0	0	0	0
1,320	1,340	115	91	69	53	38	22	7	0	0	0	0
1,340	1,360	118	94	71	55	40	24	9	0	0	0	0
1,360	1,380	121	97	74	57	42	26	11	0	0	0	0
1,380	1,400	124	100	77	59	44	28	13	0	0	0	0
1,400	1,420	127	103	80	61	46	30	15	0	0	0	0
1,420	1,440	130	106	83	63	48	32	17	1	0	0	0
1,440	1,460	133	109	86	65	50	34	19	3	0	0	0
1,460	1,480	136	112	89	67	52	36	21	5	0	0	0
1,480	1,500	139	115	92	69	54	38	23	7	0	0	0

Publication 51 (2016)

Wage Bracket Method Tables for Income Tax Withholding

MARRIED Persons—BIWEEKLY Payroll Period

(For Wages Paid through December 31, 2016)

And the wages are—		And the number of withholding allowances claimed is—										
At least	But less than	0	1	2	3	4	5	6	7	8	9	10
		The amount of income tax to be withheld is—										
$1,500	$1,520	$142	$118	$95	$71	$56	$40	$25	$9	$0	$0	$0
1,520	1,540	145	121	98	74	58	42	27	11	0	0	0
1,540	1,560	148	124	101	77	60	44	29	13	0	0	0
1,560	1,580	151	127	104	80	62	46	31	15	0	0	0
1,580	1,600	154	130	107	83	64	48	33	17	2	0	0
1,600	1,620	157	133	110	86	66	50	35	19	4	0	0
1,620	1,640	160	136	113	89	68	52	37	21	6	0	0
1,640	1,660	163	139	116	92	70	54	39	23	8	0	0
1,660	1,680	166	142	119	95	72	56	41	25	10	0	0
1,680	1,700	169	145	122	98	75	58	43	27	12	0	0
1,700	1,720	172	148	125	101	78	60	45	29	14	0	0
1,720	1,740	175	151	128	104	81	62	47	31	16	0	0
1,740	1,760	178	154	131	107	84	64	49	33	18	2	0
1,760	1,780	181	157	134	110	87	66	51	35	20	4	0
1,780	1,800	184	160	137	113	90	68	53	37	22	6	0
1,800	1,820	187	163	140	116	93	70	55	39	24	8	0
1,820	1,840	190	166	143	119	96	73	57	41	26	10	0
1,840	1,860	193	169	146	122	99	76	59	43	28	12	0
1,860	1,880	196	172	149	125	102	79	61	45	30	14	0
1,880	1,900	199	175	152	128	105	82	63	47	32	16	0
1,900	1,920	202	178	155	131	108	85	65	49	34	18	2
1,920	1,940	205	181	158	134	111	88	67	51	36	20	4
1,940	1,960	208	184	161	137	114	91	69	53	38	22	6
1,960	1,980	211	187	164	140	117	94	71	55	40	24	8
1,980	2,000	214	190	167	143	120	97	73	57	42	26	10
2,000	2,020	217	193	170	146	123	100	76	59	44	28	12
2,020	2,040	220	196	173	149	126	103	79	61	46	30	14
2,040	2,060	223	199	176	152	129	106	82	63	48	32	16
2,060	2,080	226	202	179	155	132	109	85	65	50	34	18
2,080	2,100	229	205	182	158	135	112	88	67	52	36	20
2,100	2,120	232	208	185	161	138	115	91	69	54	38	22
2,120	2,140	235	211	188	164	141	118	94	71	56	40	24
2,140	2,160	238	214	191	167	144	121	97	74	58	42	26
2,160	2,180	241	217	194	170	147	124	100	77	60	44	28
2,180	2,200	244	220	197	173	150	127	103	80	62	46	30
2,200	2,220	247	223	200	176	153	130	106	83	64	48	32
2,220	2,240	250	226	203	179	156	133	109	86	66	50	34
2,240	2,260	253	229	206	182	159	136	112	89	68	52	36
2,260	2,280	256	232	209	185	162	139	115	92	70	54	38
2,280	2,300	259	235	212	188	165	142	118	95	72	56	40
2,300	2,320	262	238	215	191	168	145	121	98	75	58	42
2,320	2,340	265	241	218	194	171	148	124	101	78	60	44
2,340	2,360	268	244	221	197	174	151	127	104	81	62	46
2,360	2,380	271	247	224	200	177	154	130	107	84	64	48
2,380	2,400	274	250	227	203	180	157	133	110	87	66	50
2,400	2,420	277	253	230	206	183	160	136	113	90	68	52
2,420	2,440	280	256	233	209	186	163	139	116	93	70	54
2,440	2,460	283	259	236	212	189	166	142	119	96	72	56
2,460	2,480	286	262	239	215	192	169	145	122	99	75	58
2,480	2,500	289	265	242	218	195	172	148	125	102	78	60
2,500	2,520	292	268	245	221	198	175	151	128	105	81	62
2,520	2,540	295	271	248	224	201	178	154	131	108	84	64
2,540	2,560	298	274	251	227	204	181	157	134	111	87	66
2,560	2,580	301	277	254	230	207	184	160	137	114	90	68
2,580	2,600	304	280	257	233	210	187	163	140	117	93	70
2,600	2,620	307	283	260	236	213	190	166	143	120	96	73
2,620	2,640	310	286	263	239	216	193	169	146	123	99	76
2,640	2,660	313	289	266	242	219	196	172	149	126	102	79
2,660	2,680	316	292	269	245	222	199	175	152	129	105	82
2,680	2,700	319	295	272	248	225	202	178	155	132	108	85
2,700	2,720	322	298	275	251	228	205	181	158	135	111	88
2,720	2,740	325	301	278	254	231	208	184	161	138	114	91
2,740	2,760	328	304	281	257	234	211	187	164	141	117	94
2,760	2,780	331	307	284	260	237	214	190	167	144	120	97
2,780	2,800	334	310	287	263	240	217	193	170	147	123	100
2,800	2,820	337	313	290	266	243	220	196	173	150	126	103
2,820	2,840	340	316	293	269	246	223	199	176	153	129	106
2,840	2,860	343	319	296	272	249	226	202	179	156	132	109
2,860	2,880	346	322	299	275	252	229	205	182	159	135	112

$2,880 and over — Use Table 2(b) for a **MARRIED person** on page 24. Also see the instructions on page 23.

Wage Bracket Method Tables for Income Tax Withholding

SINGLE Persons—SEMIMONTHLY Payroll Period

(For Wages Paid through December 31, 2016)

And the wages are–		And the number of withholding allowances claimed is—										
At least	But less than	0	1	2	3	4	5	6	7	8	9	10
		The amount of income tax to be withheld is—										
$ 0	$115	$0	$0	$0	$0	$0	$0	$0	$0	$0	$0	$0
115	120	2	0	0	0	0	0	0	0	0	0	0
120	125	3	0	0	0	0	0	0	0	0	0	0
125	130	3	0	0	0	0	0	0	0	0	0	0
130	135	4	0	0	0	0	0	0	0	0	0	0
135	140	4	0	0	0	0	0	0	0	0	0	0
140	145	5	0	0	0	0	0	0	0	0	0	0
145	150	5	0	0	0	0	0	0	0	0	0	0
150	155	6	0	0	0	0	0	0	0	0	0	0
155	160	6	0	0	0	0	0	0	0	0	0	0
160	165	7	0	0	0	0	0	0	0	0	0	0
165	170	7	0	0	0	0	0	0	0	0	0	0
170	175	8	0	0	0	0	0	0	0	0	0	0
175	180	8	0	0	0	0	0	0	0	0	0	0
180	185	9	0	0	0	0	0	0	0	0	0	0
185	190	9	0	0	0	0	0	0	0	0	0	0
190	195	10	0	0	0	0	0	0	0	0	0	0
195	200	10	0	0	0	0	0	0	0	0	0	0
200	205	11	0	0	0	0	0	0	0	0	0	0
205	210	11	0	0	0	0	0	0	0	0	0	0
210	215	12	0	0	0	0	0	0	0	0	0	0
215	220	12	0	0	0	0	0	0	0	0	0	0
220	225	13	0	0	0	0	0	0	0	0	0	0
225	230	13	0	0	0	0	0	0	0	0	0	0
230	235	14	0	0	0	0	0	0	0	0	0	0
235	240	14	0	0	0	0	0	0	0	0	0	0
240	245	15	0	0	0	0	0	0	0	0	0	0
245	250	15	0	0	0	0	0	0	0	0	0	0
250	260	16	0	0	0	0	0	0	0	0	0	0
260	270	17	0	0	0	0	0	0	0	0	0	0
270	280	18	1	0	0	0	0	0	0	0	0	0
280	290	19	2	0	0	0	0	0	0	0	0	0
290	300	20	3	0	0	0	0	0	0	0	0	0
300	310	21	4	0	0	0	0	0	0	0	0	0
310	320	22	5	0	0	0	0	0	0	0	0	0
320	330	23	6	0	0	0	0	0	0	0	0	0
330	340	24	7	0	0	0	0	0	0	0	0	0
340	350	25	8	0	0	0	0	0	0	0	0	0
350	360	26	9	0	0	0	0	0	0	0	0	0
360	370	27	10	0	0	0	0	0	0	0	0	0
370	380	28	11	0	0	0	0	0	0	0	0	0
380	390	29	12	0	0	0	0	0	0	0	0	0
390	400	30	13	0	0	0	0	0	0	0	0	0
400	410	31	14	0	0	0	0	0	0	0	0	0
410	420	32	15	0	0	0	0	0	0	0	0	0
420	430	33	16	0	0	0	0	0	0	0	0	0
430	440	34	17	0	0	0	0	0	0	0	0	0
440	450	35	18	1	0	0	0	0	0	0	0	0
450	460	36	19	2	0	0	0	0	0	0	0	0
460	470	37	20	3	0	0	0	0	0	0	0	0
470	480	38	21	4	0	0	0	0	0	0	0	0
480	490	39	22	5	0	0	0	0	0	0	0	0
490	500	41	23	6	0	0	0	0	0	0	0	0
500	520	43	25	8	0	0	0	0	0	0	0	0
520	540	46	27	10	0	0	0	0	0	0	0	0
540	560	49	29	12	0	0	0	0	0	0	0	0
560	580	52	31	14	0	0	0	0	0	0	0	0
580	600	55	33	16	0	0	0	0	0	0	0	0
600	620	58	35	18	1	0	0	0	0	0	0	0
620	640	61	37	20	3	0	0	0	0	0	0	0
640	660	64	39	22	5	0	0	0	0	0	0	0
660	680	67	42	24	7	0	0	0	0	0	0	0
680	700	70	45	26	9	0	0	0	0	0	0	0
700	720	73	48	28	11	0	0	0	0	0	0	0
720	740	76	51	30	13	0	0	0	0	0	0	0
740	760	79	54	32	15	0	0	0	0	0	0	0
760	780	82	57	34	17	0	0	0	0	0	0	0
780	800	85	60	36	19	2	0	0	0	0	0	0

Publication 51 (2016)

Wage Bracket Method Tables for Income Tax Withholding

SINGLE Persons—SEMIMONTHLY Payroll Period

(For Wages Paid through December 31, 2016)

And the wages are—		And the number of withholding allowances claimed is—										
At least	But less than	0	1	2	3	4	5	6	7	8	9	10
		The amount of income tax to be withheld is—										
$800	$820	$88	$63	$38	$21	$4	$0	$0	$0	$0	$0	$0
820	840	91	66	40	23	6	0	0	0	0	0	0
840	860	94	69	43	25	8	0	0	0	0	0	0
860	880	97	72	46	27	10	0	0	0	0	0	0
880	900	100	75	49	29	12	0	0	0	0	0	0
900	920	103	78	52	31	14	0	0	0	0	0	0
920	940	106	81	55	33	16	0	0	0	0	0	0
940	960	109	84	58	35	18	1	0	0	0	0	0
960	980	112	87	61	37	20	3	0	0	0	0	0
980	1,000	115	90	64	39	22	5	0	0	0	0	0
1,000	1,020	118	93	67	42	24	7	0	0	0	0	0
1,020	1,040	121	96	70	45	26	9	0	0	0	0	0
1,040	1,060	124	99	73	48	28	11	0	0	0	0	0
1,060	1,080	127	102	76	51	30	13	0	0	0	0	0
1,080	1,100	130	105	79	54	32	15	0	0	0	0	0
1,100	1,120	133	108	82	57	34	17	0	0	0	0	0
1,120	1,140	136	111	85	60	36	19	2	0	0	0	0
1,140	1,160	139	114	88	63	38	21	4	0	0	0	0
1,160	1,180	142	117	91	66	41	23	6	0	0	0	0
1,180	1,200	145	120	94	69	44	25	8	0	0	0	0
1,200	1,220	148	123	97	72	47	27	10	0	0	0	0
1,220	1,240	151	126	100	75	50	29	12	0	0	0	0
1,240	1,260	154	129	103	78	53	31	14	0	0	0	0
1,260	1,280	157	132	106	81	56	33	16	0	0	0	0
1,280	1,300	160	135	109	84	59	35	18	2	0	0	0
1,300	1,320	163	138	112	87	62	37	20	4	0	0	0
1,320	1,340	166	141	115	90	65	40	22	6	0	0	0
1,340	1,360	169	144	118	93	68	43	24	8	0	0	0
1,360	1,380	172	147	121	96	71	46	26	10	0	0	0
1,380	1,400	175	150	124	99	74	49	28	12	0	0	0
1,400	1,420	178	153	127	102	77	52	30	14	0	0	0
1,420	1,440	181	156	130	105	80	55	32	16	0	0	0
1,440	1,460	184	159	133	108	83	58	34	18	1	0	0
1,460	1,480	187	162	136	111	86	61	36	20	3	0	0
1,480	1,500	190	165	139	114	89	64	38	22	5	0	0
1,500	1,520	193	168	142	117	92	67	41	24	7	0	0
1,520	1,540	196	171	145	120	95	70	44	26	9	0	0
1,540	1,560	199	174	148	123	98	73	47	28	11	0	0
1,560	1,580	202	177	151	126	101	76	50	30	13	0	0
1,580	1,600	205	180	154	129	104	79	53	32	15	0	0
1,600	1,620	208	183	157	132	107	82	56	34	17	0	0
1,620	1,640	211	186	160	135	110	85	59	36	19	2	0
1,640	1,660	214	189	163	138	113	88	62	38	21	4	0
1,660	1,680	218	192	166	141	116	91	65	40	23	6	0
1,680	1,700	223	195	169	144	119	94	68	43	25	8	0
1,700	1,720	228	198	172	147	122	97	71	46	27	10	0
1,720	1,740	233	201	175	150	125	100	74	49	29	12	0
1,740	1,760	238	204	178	153	128	103	77	52	31	14	0
1,760	1,780	243	207	181	156	131	106	80	55	33	16	0
1,780	1,800	248	210	184	159	134	109	83	58	35	18	1
1,800	1,820	253	213	187	162	137	112	86	61	37	20	3
1,820	1,840	258	216	190	165	140	115	89	64	39	22	5
1,840	1,860	263	221	193	168	143	118	92	67	42	24	7
1,860	1,880	268	226	196	171	146	121	95	70	45	26	9
1,880	1,900	273	231	199	174	149	124	98	73	48	28	11
1,900	1,920	278	236	202	177	152	127	101	76	51	30	13
1,920	1,940	283	241	205	180	155	130	104	79	54	32	15
1,940	1,960	288	246	208	183	158	133	107	82	57	34	17
1,960	1,980	293	251	211	186	161	136	110	85	60	36	19
1,980	2,000	298	256	214	189	164	139	113	88	63	38	21
2,000	2,020	303	261	218	192	167	142	116	91	66	40	23
2,020	2,040	308	266	223	195	170	145	119	94	69	43	25
2,040	2,060	313	271	228	198	173	148	122	97	72	46	27
2,060	2,080	318	276	233	201	176	151	125	100	75	49	29
2,080	2,100	323	281	238	204	179	154	128	103	78	52	31
2,100	2,120	328	286	243	207	182	157	131	106	81	55	33
2,120	2,140	333	291	248	210	185	160	134	109	84	58	35

$2,140 and over — Use Table 3(a) for a **SINGLE person** on page 24. Also see the instructions on page 23.

Wage Bracket Method Tables for Income Tax Withholding

MARRIED Persons—SEMIMONTHLY Payroll Period

(For Wages Paid through December 31, 2016)

And the wages are—		And the number of withholding allowances claimed is—										
At least	But less than	0	1	2	3	4	5	6	7	8	9	10
		The amount of income tax to be withheld is—										
$ 0	$360	$0	$0	$0	$0	$0	$0	$0	$0	$0	$0	$0
360	370	1	0	0	0	0	0	0	0	0	0	0
370	380	2	0	0	0	0	0	0	0	0	0	0
380	390	3	0	0	0	0	0	0	0	0	0	0
390	400	4	0	0	0	0	0	0	0	0	0	0
400	410	5	0	0	0	0	0	0	0	0	0	0
410	420	6	0	0	0	0	0	0	0	0	0	0
420	430	7	0	0	0	0	0	0	0	0	0	0
430	440	8	0	0	0	0	0	0	0	0	0	0
440	450	9	0	0	0	0	0	0	0	0	0	0
450	460	10	0	0	0	0	0	0	0	0	0	0
460	470	11	0	0	0	0	0	0	0	0	0	0
470	480	12	0	0	0	0	0	0	0	0	0	0
480	490	13	0	0	0	0	0	0	0	0	0	0
490	500	14	0	0	0	0	0	0	0	0	0	0
500	520	15	0	0	0	0	0	0	0	0	0	0
520	540	17	1	0	0	0	0	0	0	0	0	0
540	560	19	3	0	0	0	0	0	0	0	0	0
560	580	21	5	0	0	0	0	0	0	0	0	0
580	600	23	7	0	0	0	0	0	0	0	0	0
600	620	25	9	0	0	0	0	0	0	0	0	0
620	640	27	11	0	0	0	0	0	0	0	0	0
640	660	29	13	0	0	0	0	0	0	0	0	0
660	680	31	15	0	0	0	0	0	0	0	0	0
680	700	33	17	0	0	0	0	0	0	0	0	0
700	720	35	19	2	0	0	0	0	0	0	0	0
720	740	37	21	4	0	0	0	0	0	0	0	0
740	760	39	23	6	0	0	0	0	0	0	0	0
760	780	41	25	8	0	0	0	0	0	0	0	0
780	800	43	27	10	0	0	0	0	0	0	0	0
800	820	45	29	12	0	0	0	0	0	0	0	0
820	840	47	31	14	0	0	0	0	0	0	0	0
840	860	49	33	16	0	0	0	0	0	0	0	0
860	880	51	35	18	1	0	0	0	0	0	0	0
880	900	53	37	20	3	0	0	0	0	0	0	0
900	920	55	39	22	5	0	0	0	0	0	0	0
920	940	57	41	24	7	0	0	0	0	0	0	0
940	960	59	43	26	9	0	0	0	0	0	0	0
960	980	61	45	28	11	0	0	0	0	0	0	0
980	1,000	63	47	30	13	0	0	0	0	0	0	0
1,000	1,020	65	49	32	15	0	0	0	0	0	0	0
1,020	1,040	67	51	34	17	0	0	0	0	0	0	0
1,040	1,060	69	53	36	19	2	0	0	0	0	0	0
1,060	1,080	71	55	38	21	4	0	0	0	0	0	0
1,080	1,100	73	57	40	23	6	0	0	0	0	0	0
1,100	1,120	75	59	42	25	8	0	0	0	0	0	0
1,120	1,140	77	61	44	27	10	0	0	0	0	0	0
1,140	1,160	80	63	46	29	12	0	0	0	0	0	0
1,160	1,180	83	65	48	31	14	0	0	0	0	0	0
1,180	1,200	86	67	50	33	16	0	0	0	0	0	0
1,200	1,220	89	69	52	35	18	1	0	0	0	0	0
1,220	1,240	92	71	54	37	20	3	0	0	0	0	0
1,240	1,260	95	73	56	39	22	5	0	0	0	0	0
1,260	1,280	98	75	58	41	24	7	0	0	0	0	0
1,280	1,300	101	77	60	43	26	9	0	0	0	0	0
1,300	1,320	104	79	62	45	28	11	0	0	0	0	0
1,320	1,340	107	82	64	47	30	13	0	0	0	0	0
1,340	1,360	110	85	66	49	32	15	0	0	0	0	0
1,360	1,380	113	88	68	51	34	17	0	0	0	0	0
1,380	1,400	116	91	70	53	36	19	2	0	0	0	0
1,400	1,420	119	94	72	55	38	21	4	0	0	0	0
1,420	1,440	122	97	74	57	40	23	6	0	0	0	0
1,440	1,460	125	100	76	59	42	25	8	0	0	0	0
1,460	1,480	128	103	78	61	44	27	10	0	0	0	0
1,480	1,500	131	106	81	63	46	29	12	0	0	0	0
1,500	1,520	134	109	84	65	48	31	14	0	0	0	0
1,520	1,540	137	112	87	67	50	33	16	0	0	0	0
1,540	1,560	140	115	90	69	52	35	18	1	0	0	0
1,560	1,580	143	118	93	71	54	37	20	3	0	0	0
1,580	1,600	146	121	96	73	56	39	22	5	0	0	0

Publication 51 (2016)

Wage Bracket Method Tables for Income Tax Withholding

MARRIED Persons—**SEMIMONTHLY** Payroll Period

(For Wages Paid through December 31, 2016)

And the wages are—		And the number of withholding allowances claimed is—										
At least	But less than	0	1	2	3	4	5	6	7	8	9	10
		The amount of income tax to be withheld is—										
$1,600	$1,620	$149	$124	$99	$75	$58	$41	$24	$7	$0	$0	$0
1,620	1,640	152	127	102	77	60	43	26	9	0	0	0
1,640	1,660	155	130	105	79	62	45	28	11	0	0	0
1,660	1,680	158	133	108	82	64	47	30	13	0	0	0
1,680	1,700	161	136	111	85	66	49	32	15	0	0	0
1,700	1,720	164	139	114	88	68	51	34	17	0	0	0
1,720	1,740	167	142	117	91	70	53	36	19	2	0	0
1,740	1,760	170	145	120	94	72	55	38	21	4	0	0
1,760	1,780	173	148	123	97	74	57	40	23	6	0	0
1,780	1,800	176	151	126	100	76	59	42	25	8	0	0
1,800	1,820	179	154	129	103	78	61	44	27	10	0	0
1,820	1,840	182	157	132	106	81	63	46	29	12	0	0
1,840	1,860	185	160	135	109	84	65	48	31	14	0	0
1,860	1,880	188	163	138	112	87	67	50	33	16	0	0
1,880	1,900	191	166	141	115	90	69	52	35	18	2	0
1,900	1,920	194	169	144	118	93	71	54	37	20	4	0
1,920	1,940	197	172	147	121	96	73	56	39	22	6	0
1,940	1,960	200	175	150	124	99	75	58	41	24	8	0
1,960	1,980	203	178	153	127	102	77	60	43	26	10	0
1,980	2,000	206	181	156	130	105	80	62	45	28	12	0
2,000	2,020	209	184	159	133	108	83	64	47	30	14	0
2,020	2,040	212	187	162	136	111	86	66	49	32	16	0
2,040	2,060	215	190	165	139	114	89	68	51	34	18	1
2,060	2,080	218	193	168	142	117	92	70	53	36	20	3
2,080	2,100	221	196	171	145	120	95	72	55	38	22	5
2,100	2,120	224	199	174	148	123	98	74	57	40	24	7
2,120	2,140	227	202	177	151	126	101	76	59	42	26	9
2,140	2,160	230	205	180	154	129	104	79	61	44	28	11
2,160	2,180	233	208	183	157	132	107	82	63	46	30	13
2,180	2,200	236	211	186	160	135	110	85	65	48	32	15
2,200	2,220	239	214	189	163	138	113	88	67	50	34	17
2,220	2,240	242	217	192	166	141	116	91	69	52	36	19
2,240	2,260	245	220	195	169	144	119	94	71	54	38	21
2,260	2,280	248	223	198	172	147	122	97	73	56	40	23
2,280	2,300	251	226	201	175	150	125	100	75	58	42	25
2,300	2,320	254	229	204	178	153	128	103	77	60	44	27
2,320	2,340	257	232	207	181	156	131	106	80	62	46	29
2,340	2,360	260	235	210	184	159	134	109	83	64	48	31
2,360	2,380	263	238	213	187	162	137	112	86	66	50	33
2,380	2,400	266	241	216	190	165	140	115	89	68	52	35
2,400	2,420	269	244	219	193	168	143	118	92	70	54	37
2,420	2,440	272	247	222	196	171	146	121	95	72	56	39
2,440	2,460	275	250	225	199	174	149	124	98	74	58	41
2,460	2,480	278	253	228	202	177	152	127	101	76	60	43
2,480	2,500	281	256	231	205	180	155	130	104	79	62	45
2,500	2,520	284	259	234	208	183	158	133	107	82	64	47
2,520	2,540	287	262	237	211	186	161	136	110	85	66	49
2,540	2,560	290	265	240	214	189	164	139	113	88	68	51
2,560	2,580	293	268	243	217	192	167	142	116	91	70	53
2,580	2,600	296	271	246	220	195	170	145	119	94	72	55
2,600	2,620	299	274	249	223	198	173	148	122	97	74	57
2,620	2,640	302	277	252	226	201	176	151	125	100	76	59
2,640	2,660	305	280	255	229	204	179	154	128	103	78	61
2,660	2,680	308	283	258	232	207	182	157	131	106	81	63
2,680	2,700	311	286	261	235	210	185	160	134	109	84	65
2,700	2,720	314	289	264	238	213	188	163	137	112	87	67
2,720	2,740	317	292	267	241	216	191	166	140	115	90	69
2,740	2,760	320	295	270	244	219	194	169	143	118	93	71
2,760	2,780	323	298	273	247	222	197	172	146	121	96	73
2,780	2,800	326	301	276	250	225	200	175	149	124	99	75
2,800	2,820	329	304	279	253	228	203	178	152	127	102	77
2,820	2,840	332	307	282	256	231	206	181	155	130	105	79
2,840	2,860	335	310	285	259	234	209	184	158	133	108	82
2,860	2,880	338	313	288	262	237	212	187	161	136	111	85
2,880	2,900	341	316	291	265	240	215	190	164	139	114	88
2,900	2,920	344	319	294	268	243	218	193	167	142	117	91

$2,920 and over   Use Table 3(b) for a **MARRIED person** on page 24. Also see the instructions on page 23.

Wage Bracket Method Tables for Income Tax Withholding

SINGLE Persons—**MONTHLY** Payroll Period

(For Wages Paid through December 31, 2016)

And the wages are—		And the number of withholding allowances claimed is—										
At least	But less than	0	1	2	3	4	5	6	7	8	9	10
		The amount of income tax to be withheld is—										
$ 0	$220	$0	$0	$0	$0	$0	$0	$0	$0	$0	$0	$0
220	230	4	0	0	0	0	0	0	0	0	0	0
230	240	5	0	0	0	0	0	0	0	0	0	0
240	250	6	0	0	0	0	0	0	0	0	0	0
250	260	7	0	0	0	0	0	0	0	0	0	0
260	270	8	0	0	0	0	0	0	0	0	0	0
270	280	9	0	0	0	0	0	0	0	0	0	0
280	290	10	0	0	0	0	0	0	0	0	0	0
290	300	11	0	0	0	0	0	0	0	0	0	0
300	320	12	0	0	0	0	0	0	0	0	0	0
320	340	14	0	0	0	0	0	0	0	0	0	0
340	360	16	0	0	0	0	0	0	0	0	0	0
360	380	18	0	0	0	0	0	0	0	0	0	0
380	400	20	0	0	0	0	0	0	0	0	0	0
400	420	22	0	0	0	0	0	0	0	0	0	0
420	440	24	0	0	0	0	0	0	0	0	0	0
440	460	26	0	0	0	0	0	0	0	0	0	0
460	480	28	0	0	0	0	0	0	0	0	0	0
480	500	30	0	0	0	0	0	0	0	0	0	0
500	520	32	0	0	0	0	0	0	0	0	0	0
520	540	34	1	0	0	0	0	0	0	0	0	0
540	560	36	3	0	0	0	0	0	0	0	0	0
560	580	38	5	0	0	0	0	0	0	0	0	0
580	600	40	7	0	0	0	0	0	0	0	0	0
600	640	43	10	0	0	0	0	0	0	0	0	0
640	680	47	14	0	0	0	0	0	0	0	0	0
680	720	51	18	0	0	0	0	0	0	0	0	0
720	760	55	22	0	0	0	0	0	0	0	0	0
760	800	59	26	0	0	0	0	0	0	0	0	0
800	840	63	30	0	0	0	0	0	0	0	0	0
840	880	67	34	0	0	0	0	0	0	0	0	0
880	920	71	38	4	0	0	0	0	0	0	0	0
920	960	75	42	8	0	0	0	0	0	0	0	0
960	1,000	80	46	12	0	0	0	0	0	0	0	0
1,000	1,040	86	50	16	0	0	0	0	0	0	0	0
1,040	1,080	92	54	20	0	0	0	0	0	0	0	0
1,080	1,120	98	58	24	0	0	0	0	0	0	0	0
1,120	1,160	104	62	28	0	0	0	0	0	0	0	0
1,160	1,200	110	66	32	0	0	0	0	0	0	0	0
1,200	1,240	116	70	36	2	0	0	0	0	0	0	0
1,240	1,280	122	74	40	6	0	0	0	0	0	0	0
1,280	1,320	128	78	44	10	0	0	0	0	0	0	0
1,320	1,360	134	84	48	14	0	0	0	0	0	0	0
1,360	1,400	140	90	52	18	0	0	0	0	0	0	0
1,400	1,440	146	96	56	22	0	0	0	0	0	0	0
1,440	1,480	152	102	60	26	0	0	0	0	0	0	0
1,480	1,520	158	108	64	30	0	0	0	0	0	0	0
1,520	1,560	164	114	68	34	0	0	0	0	0	0	0
1,560	1,600	170	120	72	38	4	0	0	0	0	0	0
1,600	1,640	176	126	76	42	8	0	0	0	0	0	0
1,640	1,680	182	132	81	46	12	0	0	0	0	0	0
1,680	1,720	188	138	87	50	16	0	0	0	0	0	0
1,720	1,760	194	144	93	54	20	0	0	0	0	0	0
1,760	1,800	200	150	99	58	24	0	0	0	0	0	0
1,800	1,840	206	156	105	62	28	0	0	0	0	0	0
1,840	1,880	212	162	111	66	32	0	0	0	0	0	0
1,880	1,920	218	168	117	70	36	3	0	0	0	0	0
1,920	1,960	224	174	123	74	40	7	0	0	0	0	0
1,960	2,000	230	180	129	78	44	11	0	0	0	0	0
2,000	2,040	236	186	135	84	48	15	0	0	0	0	0
2,040	2,080	242	192	141	90	52	19	0	0	0	0	0
2,080	2,120	248	198	147	96	56	23	0	0	0	0	0
2,120	2,160	254	204	153	102	60	27	0	0	0	0	0
2,160	2,200	260	210	159	108	64	31	0	0	0	0	0
2,200	2,240	266	216	165	114	68	35	1	0	0	0	0
2,240	2,280	272	222	171	120	72	39	5	0	0	0	0
2,280	2,320	278	228	177	126	76	43	9	0	0	0	0
2,320	2,360	284	234	183	132	82	47	13	0	0	0	0
2,360	2,400	290	240	189	138	88	51	17	0	0	0	0

Publication 51 (2016)

Wage Bracket Method Tables for Income Tax Withholding

SINGLE Persons—MONTHLY Payroll Period

(For Wages Paid through December 31, 2016)

And the wages are–		And the number of withholding allowances claimed is—										
At least	But less than	0	1	2	3	4	5	6	7	8	9	10
		The amount of income tax to be withheld is—										
$2,400	$2,440	$296	$246	$195	$144	$94	$55	$21	$0	$0	$0	$0
2,440	2,480	302	252	201	150	100	59	25	0	0	0	0
2,480	2,520	308	258	207	156	106	63	29	0	0	0	0
2,520	2,560	314	264	213	162	112	67	33	0	0	0	0
2,560	2,600	320	270	219	168	118	71	37	3	0	0	0
2,600	2,640	326	276	225	174	124	75	41	7	0	0	0
2,640	2,680	332	282	231	180	130	79	45	11	0	0	0
2,680	2,720	338	288	237	186	136	85	49	15	0	0	0
2,720	2,760	344	294	243	192	142	91	53	19	0	0	0
2,760	2,800	350	300	249	198	148	97	57	23	0	0	0
2,800	2,840	356	306	255	204	154	103	61	27	0	0	0
2,840	2,880	362	312	261	210	160	109	65	31	0	0	0
2,880	2,920	368	318	267	216	166	115	69	35	1	0	0
2,920	2,960	374	324	273	222	172	121	73	39	5	0	0
2,960	3,000	380	330	279	228	178	127	77	43	9	0	0
3,000	3,040	386	336	285	234	184	133	82	47	13	0	0
3,040	3,080	392	342	291	240	190	139	88	51	17	0	0
3,080	3,120	398	348	297	246	196	145	94	55	21	0	0
3,120	3,160	404	354	303	252	202	151	100	59	25	0	0
3,160	3,200	410	360	309	258	208	157	106	63	29	0	0
3,200	3,240	416	366	315	264	214	163	112	67	33	0	0
3,240	3,280	422	372	321	270	220	169	118	71	37	4	0
3,280	3,320	428	378	327	276	226	175	124	75	41	8	0
3,320	3,360	436	384	333	282	232	181	130	80	45	12	0
3,360	3,400	446	390	339	288	238	187	136	86	49	16	0
3,400	3,440	456	396	345	294	244	193	142	92	53	20	0
3,440	3,480	466	402	351	300	250	199	148	98	57	24	0
3,480	3,520	476	408	357	306	256	205	154	104	61	28	0
3,520	3,560	486	414	363	312	262	211	160	110	65	32	0
3,560	3,600	496	420	369	318	268	217	166	116	69	36	2
3,600	3,640	506	426	375	324	274	223	172	122	73	40	6
3,640	3,680	516	432	381	330	280	229	178	128	77	44	10
3,680	3,720	526	441	387	336	286	235	184	134	83	48	14
3,720	3,760	536	451	393	342	292	241	190	140	89	52	18
3,760	3,800	546	461	399	348	298	247	196	146	95	56	22
3,800	3,840	556	471	405	354	304	253	202	152	101	60	26
3,840	3,880	566	481	411	360	310	259	208	158	107	64	30
3,880	3,920	576	491	417	366	316	265	214	164	113	68	34
3,920	3,960	586	501	423	372	322	271	220	170	119	72	38
3,960	4,000	596	511	429	378	328	277	226	176	125	76	42
4,000	4,040	606	521	437	384	334	283	232	182	131	81	46
4,040	4,080	616	531	447	390	340	289	238	188	137	87	50
4,080	4,120	626	541	457	396	346	295	244	194	143	93	54
4,120	4,160	636	551	467	402	352	301	250	200	149	99	58
4,160	4,200	646	561	477	408	358	307	256	206	155	105	62
4,200	4,240	656	571	487	414	364	313	262	212	161	111	66
4,240	4,280	666	581	497	420	370	319	268	218	167	117	70
4,280	4,320	676	591	507	426	376	325	274	224	173	123	74
4,320	4,360	686	601	517	433	382	331	280	230	179	129	78
4,360	4,400	696	611	527	443	388	337	286	236	185	135	84
4,400	4,440	706	621	537	453	394	343	292	242	191	141	90
4,440	4,480	716	631	547	463	400	349	298	248	197	147	96
4,480	4,520	726	641	557	473	406	355	304	254	203	153	102
4,520	4,560	736	651	567	483	412	361	310	260	209	159	108
4,560	4,600	746	661	577	493	418	367	316	266	215	165	114
4,600	4,640	756	671	587	503	424	373	322	272	221	171	120
4,640	4,680	766	681	597	513	430	379	328	278	227	177	126
4,680	4,720	776	691	607	523	438	385	334	284	233	183	132
4,720	4,760	786	701	617	533	448	391	340	290	239	189	138
4,760	4,800	796	711	627	543	458	397	346	296	245	195	144
4,800	4,840	806	721	637	553	468	403	352	302	251	201	150
4,840	4,880	816	731	647	563	478	409	358	308	257	207	156
4,880	4,920	826	741	657	573	488	415	364	314	263	213	162
4,920	4,960	836	751	667	583	498	421	370	320	269	219	168
4,960	5,000	846	761	677	593	508	427	376	326	275	225	174
5,000	5,040	856	771	687	603	518	434	382	332	281	231	180
5,040	5,080	866	781	697	613	528	444	388	338	287	237	186

$5,080 and over   Use Table 4(a) for a **SINGLE person** on page 24. Also see the instructions on page 23.

Wage Bracket Method Tables for Income Tax Withholding

MARRIED Persons—MONTHLY Payroll Period

(For Wages Paid through December 31, 2016)

And the wages are—		And the number of withholding allowances claimed is—										
At least	But less than	0	1	2	3	4	5	6	7	8	9	10
		The amount of income tax to be withheld is—										
$0	$720	$0	$0	$0	$0	$0	$0	$0	$0	$0	$0	$0
720	760	3	0	0	0	0	0	0	0	0	0	0
760	800	7	0	0	0	0	0	0	0	0	0	0
800	840	11	0	0	0	0	0	0	0	0	0	0
840	880	15	0	0	0	0	0	0	0	0	0	0
880	920	19	0	0	0	0	0	0	0	0	0	0
920	960	23	0	0	0	0	0	0	0	0	0	0
960	1,000	27	0	0	0	0	0	0	0	0	0	0
1,000	1,040	31	0	0	0	0	0	0	0	0	0	0
1,040	1,080	35	1	0	0	0	0	0	0	0	0	0
1,080	1,120	39	5	0	0	0	0	0	0	0	0	0
1,120	1,160	43	9	0	0	0	0	0	0	0	0	0
1,160	1,200	47	13	0	0	0	0	0	0	0	0	0
1,200	1,240	51	17	0	0	0	0	0	0	0	0	0
1,240	1,280	55	21	0	0	0	0	0	0	0	0	0
1,280	1,320	59	25	0	0	0	0	0	0	0	0	0
1,320	1,360	63	29	0	0	0	0	0	0	0	0	0
1,360	1,400	67	33	0	0	0	0	0	0	0	0	0
1,400	1,440	71	37	3	0	0	0	0	0	0	0	0
1,440	1,480	75	41	7	0	0	0	0	0	0	0	0
1,480	1,520	79	45	11	0	0	0	0	0	0	0	0
1,520	1,560	83	49	15	0	0	0	0	0	0	0	0
1,560	1,600	87	53	19	0	0	0	0	0	0	0	0
1,600	1,640	91	57	23	0	0	0	0	0	0	0	0
1,640	1,680	95	61	27	0	0	0	0	0	0	0	0
1,680	1,720	99	65	31	0	0	0	0	0	0	0	0
1,720	1,760	103	69	35	2	0	0	0	0	0	0	0
1,760	1,800	107	73	39	6	0	0	0	0	0	0	0
1,800	1,840	111	77	43	10	0	0	0	0	0	0	0
1,840	1,880	115	81	47	14	0	0	0	0	0	0	0
1,880	1,920	119	85	51	18	0	0	0	0	0	0	0
1,920	1,960	123	89	55	22	0	0	0	0	0	0	0
1,960	2,000	127	93	59	26	0	0	0	0	0	0	0
2,000	2,040	131	97	63	30	0	0	0	0	0	0	0
2,040	2,080	135	101	67	34	0	0	0	0	0	0	0
2,080	2,120	139	105	71	38	4	0	0	0	0	0	0
2,120	2,160	143	109	75	42	8	0	0	0	0	0	0
2,160	2,200	147	113	79	46	12	0	0	0	0	0	0
2,200	2,240	151	117	83	50	16	0	0	0	0	0	0
2,240	2,280	155	121	87	54	20	0	0	0	0	0	0
2,280	2,320	161	125	91	58	24	0	0	0	0	0	0
2,320	2,360	167	129	95	62	28	0	0	0	0	0	0
2,360	2,400	173	133	99	66	32	0	0	0	0	0	0
2,400	2,440	179	137	103	70	36	2	0	0	0	0	0
2,440	2,480	185	141	107	74	40	6	0	0	0	0	0
2,480	2,520	191	145	111	78	44	10	0	0	0	0	0
2,520	2,560	197	149	115	82	48	14	0	0	0	0	0
2,560	2,600	203	153	119	86	52	18	0	0	0	0	0
2,600	2,640	209	158	123	90	56	22	0	0	0	0	0
2,640	2,680	215	164	127	94	60	26	0	0	0	0	0
2,680	2,720	221	170	131	98	64	30	0	0	0	0	0
2,720	2,760	227	176	135	102	68	34	0	0	0	0	0
2,760	2,800	233	182	139	106	72	38	4	0	0	0	0
2,800	2,840	239	188	143	110	76	42	8	0	0	0	0
2,840	2,880	245	194	147	114	80	46	12	0	0	0	0
2,880	2,920	251	200	151	118	84	50	16	0	0	0	0
2,920	2,960	257	206	156	122	88	54	20	0	0	0	0
2,960	3,000	263	212	162	126	92	58	24	0	0	0	0
3,000	3,040	269	218	168	130	96	62	28	0	0	0	0
3,040	3,080	275	224	174	134	100	66	32	0	0	0	0
3,080	3,120	281	230	180	138	104	70	36	3	0	0	0
3,120	3,160	287	236	186	142	108	74	40	7	0	0	0
3,160	3,200	293	242	192	146	112	78	44	11	0	0	0
3,200	3,240	299	248	198	150	116	82	48	15	0	0	0
3,240	3,280	305	254	204	154	120	86	52	19	0	0	0
3,280	3,320	311	260	210	159	124	90	56	23	0	0	0
3,320	3,360	317	266	216	165	128	94	60	27	0	0	0
3,360	3,400	323	272	222	171	132	98	64	31	0	0	0

Publication 51 (2016)

Wage Bracket Method Tables for Income Tax Withholding

MARRIED Persons—MONTHLY Payroll Period

(For Wages Paid through December 31, 2016)

And the wages are—		And the number of withholding allowances claimed is—										
At least	But less than	0	1	2	3	4	5	6	7	8	9	10
		The amount of income tax to be withheld is—										
$3,400	$3,440	$329	$278	$228	$177	$136	$102	$68	$35	$1	$0	$0
3,440	3,480	335	284	234	183	140	106	72	39	5	0	0
3,480	3,520	341	290	240	189	144	110	76	43	9	0	0
3,520	3,560	347	296	246	195	148	114	80	47	13	0	0
3,560	3,600	353	302	252	201	152	118	84	51	17	0	0
3,600	3,640	359	308	258	207	156	122	88	55	21	0	0
3,640	3,680	365	314	264	213	162	126	92	59	25	0	0
3,680	3,720	371	320	270	219	168	130	96	63	29	0	0
3,720	3,760	377	326	276	225	174	134	100	67	33	0	0
3,760	3,800	383	332	282	231	180	138	104	71	37	3	0
3,800	3,840	389	338	288	237	186	142	108	75	41	7	0
3,840	3,880	395	344	294	243	192	146	112	79	45	11	0
3,880	3,920	401	350	300	249	198	150	116	83	49	15	0
3,920	3,960	407	356	306	255	204	154	120	87	53	19	0
3,960	4,000	413	362	312	261	210	160	124	91	57	23	0
4,000	4,040	419	368	318	267	216	166	128	95	61	27	0
4,040	4,080	425	374	324	273	222	172	132	99	65	31	0
4,080	4,120	431	380	330	279	228	178	136	103	69	35	1
4,120	4,160	437	386	336	285	234	184	140	107	73	39	5
4,160	4,200	443	392	342	291	240	190	144	111	77	43	9
4,200	4,240	449	398	348	297	246	196	148	115	81	47	13
4,240	4,280	455	404	354	303	252	202	152	119	85	51	17
4,280	4,320	461	410	360	309	258	208	157	123	89	55	21
4,320	4,360	467	416	366	315	264	214	163	127	93	59	25
4,360	4,400	473	422	372	321	270	220	169	131	97	63	29
4,400	4,440	479	428	378	327	276	226	175	135	101	67	33
4,440	4,480	485	434	384	333	282	232	181	139	105	71	37
4,480	4,520	491	440	390	339	288	238	187	143	109	75	41
4,520	4,560	497	446	396	345	294	244	193	147	113	79	45
4,560	4,600	503	452	402	351	300	250	199	151	117	83	49
4,600	4,640	509	458	408	357	306	256	205	155	121	87	53
4,640	4,680	515	464	414	363	312	262	211	160	125	91	57
4,680	4,720	521	470	420	369	318	268	217	166	129	95	61
4,720	4,760	527	476	426	375	324	274	223	172	133	99	65
4,760	4,800	533	482	432	381	330	280	229	178	137	103	69
4,800	4,840	539	488	438	387	336	286	235	184	141	107	73
4,840	4,880	545	494	444	393	342	292	241	190	145	111	77
4,880	4,920	551	500	450	399	348	298	247	196	149	115	81
4,920	4,960	557	506	456	405	354	304	253	202	153	119	85
4,960	5,000	563	512	462	411	360	310	259	208	158	123	89
5,000	5,040	569	518	468	417	366	316	265	214	164	127	93
5,040	5,080	575	524	474	423	372	322	271	220	170	131	97
5,080	5,120	581	530	480	429	378	328	277	226	176	135	101
5,120	5,160	587	536	486	435	384	334	283	232	182	139	105
5,160	5,200	593	542	492	441	390	340	289	238	188	143	109
5,200	5,240	599	548	498	447	396	346	295	244	194	147	113
5,240	5,280	605	554	504	453	402	352	301	250	200	151	117
5,280	5,320	611	560	510	459	408	358	307	256	206	155	121
5,320	5,360	617	566	516	465	414	364	313	262	212	161	125
5,360	5,400	623	572	522	471	420	370	319	268	218	167	129
5,400	5,440	629	578	528	477	426	376	325	274	224	173	133
5,440	5,480	635	584	534	483	432	382	331	280	230	179	137
5,480	5,520	641	590	540	489	438	388	337	286	236	185	141
5,520	5,560	647	596	546	495	444	394	343	292	242	191	145
5,560	5,600	653	602	552	501	450	400	349	298	248	197	149
5,600	5,640	659	608	558	507	456	406	355	304	254	203	153
5,640	5,680	665	614	564	513	462	412	361	310	260	209	159
5,680	5,720	671	620	570	519	468	418	367	316	266	215	165
5,720	5,760	677	626	576	525	474	424	373	322	272	221	171
5,760	5,800	683	632	582	531	480	430	379	328	278	227	177
5,800	5,840	689	638	588	537	486	436	385	334	284	233	183
5,840	5,880	695	644	594	543	492	442	391	340	290	239	189
5,880	5,920	701	650	600	549	498	448	397	346	296	245	195
5,920	5,960	707	656	606	555	504	454	403	352	302	251	201
5,960	6,000	713	662	612	561	510	460	409	358	308	257	207
6,000	6,040	719	668	618	567	516	466	415	364	314	263	213
6,040	6,080	725	674	624	573	522	472	421	370	320	269	219
6,080	6,120	731	680	630	579	528	478	427	376	326	275	225

$6,120 and over   Use Table 4(b) for a **MARRIED person** on page 24. Also see the instructions on page 23.

Wage Bracket Method Tables for Income Tax Withholding

SINGLE Persons—DAILY Payroll Period

(For Wages Paid through December 31, 2016)

And the wages are—		And the number of withholding allowances claimed is—										
At least	But less than	0	1	2	3	4	5	6	7	8	9	10
		The amount of income tax to be withheld is—										
$0	$15	$0	$0	$0	$0	$0	$0	$0	$0	$0	$0	$0
15	18	1	0	0	0	0	0	0	0	0	0	0
18	21	1	0	0	0	0	0	0	0	0	0	0
21	24	1	0	0	0	0	0	0	0	0	0	0
24	27	2	0	0	0	0	0	0	0	0	0	0
27	30	2	0	0	0	0	0	0	0	0	0	0
30	33	2	1	0	0	0	0	0	0	0	0	0
33	36	3	1	0	0	0	0	0	0	0	0	0
36	39	3	1	0	0	0	0	0	0	0	0	0
39	42	3	2	0	0	0	0	0	0	0	0	0
42	45	3	2	0	0	0	0	0	0	0	0	0
45	48	4	2	1	0	0	0	0	0	0	0	0
48	51	4	3	1	0	0	0	0	0	0	0	0
51	54	5	3	1	0	0	0	0	0	0	0	0
54	57	5	3	2	0	0	0	0	0	0	0	0
57	60	6	3	2	0	0	0	0	0	0	0	0
60	63	6	4	2	1	0	0	0	0	0	0	0
63	66	7	4	2	1	0	0	0	0	0	0	0
66	69	7	5	3	1	0	0	0	0	0	0	0
69	72	7	5	3	2	0	0	0	0	0	0	0
72	75	8	6	3	2	0	0	0	0	0	0	0
75	78	8	6	4	2	1	0	0	0	0	0	0
78	81	9	7	4	2	1	0	0	0	0	0	0
81	84	9	7	5	3	1	0	0	0	0	0	0
84	87	10	7	5	3	1	0	0	0	0	0	0
87	90	10	8	6	3	2	0	0	0	0	0	0
90	93	11	8	6	4	2	0	0	0	0	0	0
93	96	11	9	6	4	2	1	0	0	0	0	0
96	99	12	9	7	5	3	1	0	0	0	0	0
99	102	12	10	7	5	3	1	0	0	0	0	0
102	105	12	10	8	5	3	2	0	0	0	0	0
105	108	13	11	8	6	4	2	0	0	0	0	0
108	111	13	11	9	6	4	2	1	0	0	0	0
111	114	14	11	9	7	4	3	1	0	0	0	0
114	117	14	12	10	7	5	3	1	0	0	0	0
117	120	15	12	10	8	5	3	2	0	0	0	0
120	123	15	13	10	8	6	3	2	0	0	0	0
123	126	16	13	11	9	6	4	2	1	0	0	0
126	129	16	14	11	9	7	4	3	1	0	0	0
129	132	16	14	12	9	7	5	3	1	0	0	0
132	135	17	15	12	10	8	5	3	2	0	0	0
135	138	17	15	13	10	8	6	3	2	0	0	0
138	141	18	16	13	11	8	6	4	2	1	0	0
141	144	18	16	14	11	9	7	4	2	1	0	0
144	147	19	16	14	12	9	7	5	3	1	0	0
147	150	19	17	15	12	10	8	5	3	2	0	0
150	153	20	17	15	13	10	8	6	3	2	0	0
153	156	20	18	15	13	11	8	6	4	2	1	0
156	159	21	18	16	14	11	9	7	4	2	1	0
159	162	22	19	16	14	12	9	7	5	3	1	0
162	165	22	19	17	14	12	10	7	5	3	1	0
165	168	23	20	17	15	13	10	8	6	3	2	0
168	171	24	20	18	15	13	11	8	6	4	2	1
171	174	25	21	18	16	13	11	9	6	4	2	1
174	177	25	22	19	16	14	12	9	7	5	3	1
177	180	26	22	19	17	14	12	10	7	5	3	1
180	183	27	23	19	17	15	12	10	8	5	3	2
183	186	28	24	20	18	15	13	11	8	6	4	2
186	189	28	25	21	18	16	13	11	9	6	4	2
189	192	29	25	21	18	16	14	11	9	7	4	3
192	195	30	26	22	19	17	14	12	10	7	5	3
195	198	31	27	23	19	17	15	12	10	8	5	3
198	201	31	28	24	20	17	15	13	10	8	6	4
201	204	32	28	24	21	18	16	13	11	9	6	4
204	207	33	29	25	21	18	16	14	11	9	7	4
207	210	34	30	26	22	19	17	14	12	10	7	5
210	213	34	31	27	23	19	17	15	12	10	8	5
213	216	35	31	27	24	20	17	15	13	10	8	6
216	219	36	32	28	24	20	18	16	13	11	9	6
219	222	37	33	29	25	21	18	16	14	11	9	7
222	225	37	34	30	26	22	19	16	14	12	9	7

Publication 51 (2016)

Wage Bracket Method Tables for Income Tax Withholding

SINGLE Persons—DAILY Payroll Period

(For Wages Paid through December 31, 2016)

And the wages are—		And the number of withholding allowances claimed is—										
At least	But less than	0	1	2	3	4	5	6	7	8	9	10
		The amount of income tax to be withheld is—										
$225	$228	$38	$34	$30	$27	$23	$19	$17	$15	$12	$10	$8
228	231	39	35	31	27	23	20	17	15	13	10	8
231	234	40	36	32	28	24	20	18	15	13	11	8
234	237	40	37	33	29	25	21	18	16	14	11	9
237	240	41	37	33	30	26	22	19	16	14	12	9
240	243	42	38	34	30	26	22	19	17	14	12	10
243	246	43	39	35	31	27	23	20	17	15	13	10
246	249	43	40	36	32	28	24	20	18	15	13	11
249	252	44	40	36	33	29	25	21	18	16	13	11
252	255	45	41	37	33	29	25	22	19	16	14	12
255	258	46	42	38	34	30	26	22	19	17	14	12
258	261	46	43	39	35	31	27	23	19	17	15	12
261	264	47	43	39	36	32	28	24	20	18	15	13
264	267	48	44	40	36	32	28	25	21	18	16	13
267	270	49	45	41	37	33	29	25	21	19	16	14
270	273	49	46	42	38	34	30	26	22	19	17	14
273	276	50	46	42	39	35	31	27	23	19	17	15
276	279	51	47	43	39	35	31	28	24	20	18	15
279	282	52	48	44	40	36	32	28	24	21	18	16
282	285	52	49	45	41	37	33	29	25	21	18	16
285	288	53	49	45	42	38	34	30	26	22	19	17
288	291	54	50	46	42	38	34	31	27	23	19	17
291	294	55	51	47	43	39	35	31	27	24	20	17
294	297	55	52	48	44	40	36	32	28	24	20	18
297	300	56	52	48	45	41	37	33	29	25	21	18
300	303	57	53	49	45	41	37	34	30	26	22	19
303	306	58	54	50	46	42	38	34	30	27	23	19
306	309	58	55	51	47	43	39	35	31	27	23	20
309	312	59	55	51	48	44	40	36	32	28	24	20
312	315	60	56	52	48	44	40	37	33	29	25	21
315	318	61	57	53	49	45	41	37	33	30	26	22
318	321	61	58	54	50	46	42	38	34	30	26	23
321	324	62	58	54	51	47	43	39	35	31	27	23
324	327	63	59	55	51	47	43	40	36	32	28	24
327	330	64	60	56	52	48	44	40	36	33	29	25
330	333	64	61	57	53	49	45	41	37	33	29	26
333	336	65	61	57	54	50	46	42	38	34	30	26
336	339	66	62	58	54	50	46	43	39	35	31	27
339	341	67	63	59	55	51	47	43	39	35	32	28
341	343	67	63	59	55	51	48	44	40	36	32	28
343	345	68	64	60	56	52	48	44	40	36	33	29
345	347	68	64	60	56	52	49	45	41	37	33	29
347	349	69	65	61	57	53	49	45	41	37	34	30
349	351	69	65	61	57	53	50	46	42	38	34	30
351	353	70	66	62	58	54	50	46	42	38	35	31
353	355	70	66	62	58	54	51	47	43	39	35	31
355	357	71	67	63	59	55	51	47	43	39	36	32
357	359	71	67	63	59	55	52	48	44	40	36	32
359	361	72	68	64	60	56	52	48	44	40	37	33
361	363	72	68	64	60	56	53	49	45	41	37	33
363	365	73	69	65	61	57	53	49	45	41	38	34
365	367	73	69	65	61	57	54	50	46	42	38	34
367	369	74	70	66	62	58	54	50	46	42	39	35
369	371	74	70	66	62	58	55	51	47	43	39	35
371	373	75	71	67	63	59	55	51	47	43	40	36
373	375	76	71	67	63	59	56	52	48	44	40	36
375	377	76	72	68	64	60	56	52	48	44	41	37
377	379	77	72	68	64	60	57	53	49	45	41	37
379	381	77	73	69	65	61	57	53	49	45	42	38
381	383	78	73	69	65	61	58	54	50	46	42	38
383	385	78	74	70	66	62	58	54	50	46	43	39
385	387	79	75	70	66	62	59	55	51	47	43	39
387	389	79	75	71	67	63	59	55	51	47	44	40
389	391	80	76	71	67	63	60	56	52	48	44	40
391	393	81	76	72	68	64	60	56	52	48	45	41

$393 and over   Use Table 8(a) for a **SINGLE person** on page 25. Also see the instructions on page 23.

Wage Bracket Method Tables for Income Tax Withholding

MARRIED Persons—DAILY Payroll Period

(For Wages Paid through December 31, 2016)

And the wages are—		And the number of withholding allowances claimed is—										
At least	But less than	0	1	2	3	4	5	6	7	8	9	10
		The amount of income tax to be withheld is—										
$0	$39	$0	$0	$0	$0	$0	$0	$0	$0	$0	$0	$0
39	42	1	0	0	0	0	0	0	0	0	0	0
42	45	1	0	0	0	0	0	0	0	0	0	0
45	48	1	0	0	0	0	0	0	0	0	0	0
48	51	2	0	0	0	0	0	0	0	0	0	0
51	54	2	0	0	0	0	0	0	0	0	0	0
54	57	2	1	0	0	0	0	0	0	0	0	0
57	60	3	1	0	0	0	0	0	0	0	0	0
60	63	3	1	0	0	0	0	0	0	0	0	0
63	66	3	2	0	0	0	0	0	0	0	0	0
66	69	3	2	0	0	0	0	0	0	0	0	0
69	72	4	2	1	0	0	0	0	0	0	0	0
72	75	4	3	1	0	0	0	0	0	0	0	0
75	78	4	3	1	0	0	0	0	0	0	0	0
78	81	5	3	2	0	0	0	0	0	0	0	0
81	84	5	3	2	0	0	0	0	0	0	0	0
84	87	5	4	2	1	0	0	0	0	0	0	0
87	90	6	4	2	1	0	0	0	0	0	0	0
90	93	6	4	3	1	0	0	0	0	0	0	0
93	96	6	5	3	1	0	0	0	0	0	0	0
96	99	6	5	3	2	0	0	0	0	0	0	0
99	102	7	5	4	2	1	0	0	0	0	0	0
102	105	7	6	4	2	1	0	0	0	0	0	0
105	108	7	6	4	3	1	0	0	0	0	0	0
108	111	8	6	5	3	1	0	0	0	0	0	0
111	114	8	6	5	3	2	0	0	0	0	0	0
114	117	9	7	5	4	2	0	0	0	0	0	0
117	120	9	7	5	4	2	1	0	0	0	0	0
120	123	10	7	6	4	3	1	0	0	0	0	0
123	126	10	8	6	4	3	1	0	0	0	0	0
126	129	11	8	6	5	3	2	0	0	0	0	0
129	132	11	9	7	5	4	2	0	0	0	0	0
132	135	12	9	7	5	4	2	1	0	0	0	0
135	138	12	10	7	6	4	3	1	0	0	0	0
138	141	12	10	8	6	4	3	1	0	0	0	0
141	144	13	11	8	6	5	3	2	0	0	0	0
144	147	13	11	9	7	5	3	2	0	0	0	0
147	150	14	11	9	7	5	4	2	1	0	0	0
150	153	14	12	10	7	6	4	3	1	0	0	0
153	156	15	12	10	8	6	4	3	1	0	0	0
156	159	15	13	10	8	6	5	3	2	0	0	0
159	162	16	13	11	9	7	5	3	2	0	0	0
162	165	16	14	11	9	7	5	4	2	1	0	0
165	168	16	14	12	9	7	6	4	2	1	0	0
168	171	17	15	12	10	8	6	4	3	1	0	0
171	174	17	15	13	10	8	6	5	3	2	0	0
174	177	18	15	13	11	8	6	5	3	2	0	0
177	180	18	16	14	11	9	7	5	4	2	1	0
180	183	19	16	14	12	9	7	6	4	2	1	0
183	186	19	17	15	12	10	7	6	4	3	1	0
186	189	20	17	15	13	10	8	6	5	3	1	0
189	192	20	18	15	13	11	8	6	5	3	2	0
192	195	21	18	16	14	11	9	7	5	4	2	0
195	198	21	19	16	14	12	9	7	5	4	2	1
198	201	21	19	17	14	12	10	7	6	4	3	1
201	204	22	20	17	15	13	10	8	6	5	3	1
204	207	22	20	18	15	13	11	8	6	5	3	2
207	210	23	20	18	16	13	11	9	7	5	4	2
210	213	23	21	19	16	14	12	9	7	5	4	2
213	216	24	21	19	17	14	12	10	7	6	4	3
216	219	24	22	19	17	15	12	10	8	6	4	3
219	222	25	22	20	18	15	13	11	8	6	5	3
222	225	25	23	20	18	16	13	11	9	7	5	3
225	228	25	23	21	18	16	14	11	9	7	5	4
228	231	26	24	21	19	17	14	12	10	7	6	4
231	234	26	24	22	19	17	15	12	10	8	6	4
234	237	27	24	22	20	17	15	13	10	8	6	5
237	240	27	25	23	20	18	16	13	11	9	7	5
240	243	28	25	23	21	18	16	14	11	9	7	5
243	246	28	26	24	21	19	16	14	12	9	7	6
246	249	29	26	24	22	19	17	15	12	10	8	6

 Publication 51 (2016)

Wage Bracket Method Tables for Income Tax Withholding

MARRIED Persons—DAILY Payroll Period

(For Wages Paid through December 31, 2016)

And the wages are–		And the number of withholding allowances claimed is—										
At least	But less than	0	1	2	3	4	5	6	7	8	9	10
		The amount of income tax to be withheld is—										
$249	$252	$29	$27	$24	$22	$20	$17	$15	$13	$10	$8	$6
252	255	30	27	25	23	20	18	16	13	11	8	6
255	258	30	28	25	23	21	18	16	14	11	9	7
258	261	30	28	26	23	21	19	16	14	12	9	7
261	264	31	29	26	24	22	19	17	15	12	10	8
264	267	31	29	27	24	22	20	17	15	13	10	8
267	270	32	29	27	25	22	20	18	15	13	11	8
270	273	32	30	28	25	23	21	18	16	14	11	9
273	276	33	30	28	26	23	21	19	16	14	12	9
276	279	33	31	28	26	24	21	19	17	14	12	10
279	282	34	31	29	27	24	22	20	17	15	13	10
282	285	34	32	29	27	25	22	20	18	15	13	11
285	288	34	32	30	27	25	23	20	18	16	13	11
288	291	35	33	30	28	26	23	21	19	16	14	12
291	294	35	33	31	28	26	24	21	19	17	14	12
294	297	36	33	31	29	26	24	22	19	17	15	12
297	300	36	34	32	29	27	25	22	20	18	15	13
300	303	37	34	32	30	27	25	23	20	18	16	13
303	306	37	35	33	30	28	25	23	21	18	16	14
306	309	38	35	33	31	28	26	24	21	19	17	14
309	312	38	36	33	31	29	26	24	22	19	17	15
312	315	39	36	34	32	29	27	25	22	20	17	15
315	318	39	37	34	32	30	27	25	23	20	18	16
318	321	39	37	35	32	30	28	25	23	21	18	16
321	324	40	38	35	33	31	28	26	24	21	19	17
324	327	41	38	36	33	31	29	26	24	22	19	17
327	330	41	38	36	34	31	29	27	24	22	20	17
330	333	42	39	37	34	32	30	27	25	23	20	18
333	336	43	39	37	35	32	30	28	25	23	21	18
336	339	44	40	37	35	33	30	28	26	23	21	19
339	341	44	40	38	35	33	31	28	26	24	21	19
341	343	45	41	38	36	33	31	29	26	24	22	19
343	345	45	41	38	36	34	31	29	27	24	22	20
345	347	46	42	39	36	34	32	29	27	25	22	20
347	349	46	42	39	37	34	32	30	27	25	23	20
349	351	47	43	39	37	35	32	30	28	25	23	21
351	353	47	43	40	37	35	33	30	28	26	23	21
353	355	48	44	40	38	35	33	31	28	26	24	21
355	357	48	44	40	38	36	33	31	29	26	24	22
357	359	49	45	41	38	36	34	31	29	27	24	22
359	361	49	45	41	38	36	34	31	29	27	24	22
361	363	50	46	42	39	36	34	32	29	27	25	22
363	365	50	46	42	39	37	34	32	30	27	25	23
365	367	51	47	43	39	37	35	32	30	28	25	23
367	369	51	47	43	40	37	35	33	30	28	26	23
369	371	52	48	44	40	38	35	33	31	28	26	24
371	373	52	48	44	41	38	36	33	31	29	26	24
373	375	53	49	45	41	38	36	34	31	29	27	24
375	377	53	49	45	42	39	36	34	32	29	27	25
377	379	54	50	46	42	39	37	34	32	30	27	25
379	381	54	50	46	43	39	37	34	32	30	27	25
381	383	55	51	47	43	39	37	35	32	30	28	25
383	385	55	51	47	44	40	37	35	33	30	28	26
385	387	56	52	48	44	40	38	35	33	31	28	26
387	389	56	52	48	45	41	38	36	33	31	29	26
389	391	57	53	49	45	41	38	36	34	31	29	27
391	393	57	53	49	46	42	39	36	34	32	29	27
393	395	58	54	50	46	42	39	37	34	32	30	27
395	397	58	54	50	47	43	39	37	35	32	30	28
397	399	59	55	51	47	43	40	37	35	33	30	28
399	401	59	55	51	48	44	40	37	35	33	30	28
401	403	60	56	52	48	44	40	38	35	33	31	28
403	405	60	56	52	49	45	41	38	36	33	31	29
405	407	61	57	53	49	45	41	38	36	34	31	29
407	409	61	57	53	50	46	42	39	36	34	32	29

$409 and over   Use Table 8(b) for a **MARRIED person** on page 25. Also see the instructions on page 23.

How To Get Tax Help

If you have questions about a tax issue, need help preparing your tax return, or want to download free publications, forms, or instructions, go to IRS.gov and find resources that can help you right away.

Preparing and filing your tax return. Go to IRS.gov and click on the Filing tab to see your options.

 Getting answers to your tax law questions. On IRS.gov, get answers to your tax questions anytime, anywhere.

- Go to _www.irs.gov/Help-&-Resources_ for a variety of tools that will help you with your taxes.
- Additionally, you may be able to access tax law information in your electronic filing software.

Tax forms and publications. You can download or print some of the forms and publications you may need on _www.irs.gov/formspubs_. Otherwise, you can go to _www.irs.gov/orderforms_ to place an order and have forms mailed to you. You should receive your order within 10 business days.

Getting a transcript or copy of a return.

- Go to IRS.gov and click on "Get Transcript of Your Tax Records" under "Tools."
- Call the transcript toll-free line at 1-800-908-9946.
- Mail Form 4506-T (transcript request) or Form 4506 (copy of return) to the IRS.

Understanding identity theft issues.

- Go to _www.irs.gov/uac/Identity-Protection_ for information and videos.
- If you suspect you are a victim of tax-related identity theft, visit _www.irs.gov/identitytheft_ to learn what steps you should take.

Making a tax payment. The IRS uses the latest encryption technology so electronic payments are safe and secure. You can make electronic payments online, by phone, or from a mobile device. Paying electronically is quick, easy, and faster than mailing in a check or money order. Go to _www.irs.gov/payments_ to make a payment using any of the following options.

- **Debit or credit card** (approved payment processors online or by phone).
- **Electronic Funds Withdrawal** (available during _e-file_).
- **Electronic Federal Tax Payment System** (best option for businesses; enrollment required).
- **Check or money order**.

IRS2Go provides access to mobile-friendly payment options. Simply download IRS2Go from Google Play, the Apple App Store, or the Amazon Appstore, and make your payments anytime, anywhere.

What if I can't pay now? Click on the "Pay Your Tax Bill" icon on IRS.gov for more information about these additional options.

- Apply for an _online payment agreement_ to meet your tax obligation in monthly installments if you cannot pay your taxes in full today. Once you complete the online process, you will receive immediate notification of whether your agreement has been approved.
- An offer in compromise allows you to settle your tax debt for less than the full amount you owe. Use the _Offer in Compromise Pre-Qualifier_ to confirm your eligibility.

Understanding an IRS notice or letter. Enter "Understanding your notice" in the search box on IRS.gov to find additional information about your IRS notice or letter.

Visiting the IRS. Locate the nearest Taxpayer Assistance Center using the Office Locator tool on IRS.gov. Enter "office locator" in the search box. Or choose the "Contact Us" option on the IRS2Go app and search Local Offices. Before you visit, use the Locator tool to check hours and services available.

Watching IRS videos. The IRS Video portal _www.irsvideos.gov_ contains video and audio presentations for individuals, small businesses, and tax professionals. You'll find video clips of tax topics, archived versions of panel discussions and Webinars, and audio archives of tax practitioner phone forums.

Getting tax information in other languages. For taxpayers whose native language is not English, we have the following resources available.

1. Taxpayers can find information on IRS.gov in the following languages.
   a. _Spanish_.
   b. _Chinese_.
   c. _Vietnamese_.
   d. _Korean_.
   e. _Russian_.
2. The IRS Taxpayer Assistance Centers provide over-the-phone interpreter service in over 170 languages, and the service is available free to taxpayers.

The Taxpayer Advocate Service Is Here To Help You

What is the Taxpayer Advocate Service?

The Taxpayer Advocate Service (TAS) is an _independent_ organization within the Internal Revenue Service that helps taxpayers and protects taxpayer rights. Our job is to ensure that every taxpayer is treated fairly and that you know and understand your rights under the *Taxpayer Bill of Rights*.

What Can the Taxpayer Advocate Service Do For You?

We can help you resolve problems that you can't resolve with the IRS. And our service is free. If you qualify for our assistance, you will be assigned to one advocate who will work with you throughout the process and will do everything possible to resolve your issue. TAS can help you if:

- Your problem is causing financial difficulty for you, your family, or your business,
- You face (or your business is facing) an immediate threat of adverse action, or
- You've tried repeatedly to contact the IRS but no one has responded, or the IRS hasn't responded by the date promised.

How Can You Reach Us?

We have offices *in every state, the District of Columbia, and Puerto Rico*. Your local advocate's number is in your local directory and at *www.taxpayeradvocate.irs.gov*. You can also call us at 1-877-777-4778.

How Can You Learn About Your Taxpayer Rights?

The Taxpayer Bill of Rights describes ten basic rights that all taxpayers have when dealing with the IRS. Our Tax Toolkit at *www.taxpayeradvocate.irs.gov* can help you understand *what these rights mean to you* and how they apply. These are **your** rights. Know them. Use them.

How Else Does the Taxpayer Advocate Service Help Taxpayers?

TAS works to resolve large-scale problems that affect many taxpayers. If you know of one of these broad issues, please report it to us at *www.irs.gov/sams*.

Index

To help us develop a more useful index, please let us know if you have ideas for index entries. See "Comments and Suggestions" in the "Introduction" for the ways you can reach us.